"To quote Lori Armitage: 'A V ___
copy of *Women Let's Rise* has fou ___ t
me when I tell you it was not by ___ ___ ___ ___ is
an inspirational read and a powerful reminder that when women
come together to share their stumbles and their victories, they are
able to use their collective strength to elevate women worldwide.
This is how we change the world, and change the way the world
perceives the true strength of the woman."
                    -Charleyne Oulton, Royal Canadian Navy,
        author of ten publications most recently *She's No Longer Silent*
            #coachcharleybrown | www.coachcharleybrown.com

"There is nothing more inspiring than knowing you are not
alone with your fears, doubts, and dreams. This book has a unique
and perfect chapter that can fit any reader. There are tears, laugh-
ter, conflict, inspiration, and also research. As a woman and entrepreneur, I feel ready to rise!"
                    -Lucia Yglesias, lifestyle photographer and journalist
            www.luciayphotography.com | ig: @luciayphotography

"Thank you for this amazing collection of female entrepreneurs
sharing their very personal stories to help others fuel their passion
and get their message out into the world. Every inspiring chapter
of this book reveals tantalizing insight into the real story behind
each successful businesswoman. I loved reading about that pivotal
moment that launched them into superstardom and their future
success. A must-read for anyone who is unsure of how to move forward with a dream of creating and launching their own business."
                    -Karen Anderson, Author of the #1 Bestselling book,
            The Amazing Afterlife of Animals and *Hear All Creatures*

"Janet Miller's beautiful passage in the book *Women Let's Rise*, reminds women across the world of their power within and it all starts with self-love. 'Lighting the road to self-love' tells her story of how meditation and discovering the peace within was her way forward into a place of love and acceptance. And it can be yours too. There's no better time for all women of the world to rise up, expand their consciousness and allow their deep love to shine. Janet leads the way with her torch brightly shining."

-Jason Stephenson, Master Teacher of the *Empowered Sleep Formula* and Co-Author of *Success Mastery*

"*Women Let's Rise* is an incredible testament to the power of storytelling and shared experiences. This collection of inspiring stories lets all women know there is unlimited power in our collective experience. WE are powerful if we choose to believe it. WE get to change the narrative and this is evident in our stories of triumph. This book is an important tool in finding our own powerful voices and lifting up the voices of other women. Together we learn, together we grow, and together we rise."

-Dianne Bondy, Author of *Yoga For Everyone* and *Yoga Where You Are*
Diannebondyyoga.com | ig: @diannebondyyogaofficial

"This collection of stories, insights, and advice truly has something for everyone. I was blown away by the candour of these women to bare their truths and imperfections, in order to lay the groundwork for others to learn from their journeys. The diversity of perspectives is only surpassed in its brilliance by the quality of advice and guidance these women provide. One thread is apparent through this entire book—it is never too late, we all have the power to create our new reality."

-Jillian Svensson, Executive Director of SheIS
www.sheissport.com

"The extraordinary stories and life lessons shared in this book unveil a timeless truth, that a woman's beauty lies in her creative spirit, resilience, and remarkable ability to transform pain into power."

-Halima Al-Hatimy, Founder of FemCare,
host of *Mastering Menstruation* Podcast
www.femcarechi.com

"Inspiring, empowering, and beautifully written are the words that come to me after reading *Women Let's Rise*. It made me feel that no matter what these women have gone through in their lives they all found the strength to overcome and prevail no matter what their situations and or circumstances are. It's comforting to see the recurring theme in a lot of these stories fall along the lines of trusting your inner knowing and powers as well as relying on the support from other like minded women."

-Jamelia Gregory, Founder of Awakening the Woman Within
ig: @awakening_the_woman_within

"The magnitude and scope of what these young women are creating and putting into action is beyond inspirational. Our future looks brighter because of their wisdom, power, and intelligence."

-Atherton Drenth, Author of *The Intuitive Dance*
and *Following Body Wisdom*
www.athertondrenth.ca | fb: @AthertonDrenth-Author

"I'm bookmarking multiple chapters, to read again and again to further the success of my career as a business woman. It's heartwarming and motivating to work with women that *can* work together and believe in the benefit of rising in unity—there is room for everyone."

-Ky-Lee Hanson, award winning publisher, bosswoman
@kylee.hanson.bosswoman

WOMEN LET'S RISE

GOLDEN BRICK ROAD
PUBLISHING HOUSE

TABLE OF CONTENTS

World: Lead as Women Together

FOREWORD

Violette de Ayala

Founder of FemCity® and International Best Selling Author of *The Self-Guided Guru, Life Lessons for the Everyday Human*

When women share stories of their personal journeys, a world of shifts and pivots occurs based on the inspiration it holds for women creating their path of purpose and intent. Encouraging women to share their truths, falls, and risings gives permission to other women to continue on their avenues of dreams, follow their intuition, and create a life of positive impact and legacy.

Women Let's Rise shares the intimate stories of diverse women, their rise from phases of change, unpredictable times, and life altering moments to the breakthroughs and accelerations to the achieved successes in their lives. Monumental times filled with seemingly dark themes, grace, re-alignment, and triumphs can create the outcome and be the gift that shines our talents and purpose in this world.

It's through story-telling with pure vulnerability and authenticity that transitional scenarios of pain or confusion can be used to inspire, motivate, and uplift those around us or those simply witnessing our vignette of life. I can attest that the stories of other women who rose to their grandest vision, purpose, and best selves, inspired me to create, go beyond, and continue to live and share my story of rising.

Women Let's Rise takes you in, giving you the avenues of leveraging stories to pivot into your own grandest vision, develop the courage to move forward, and step into the bravery to design your life with abundance, wealth, and harmonious connectivity to others.

When one woman rises, and intentionally elevates all the other women around her, they all then rise together to greater heights. When women rise up together, the world shines brighter. It also reminds us to pull each other up, be there for one another, and that there is space at the top for all women to lead together.

INTRODUCTION

Lola T. Small

"The future is female."

We hear this saying a lot today in our social and political arenas, rallying people around the idea that women are here to take over the world. Whatever your interpretation or views of this movement, one thing is clear: the status of women in our traditionally male-dominated societies is shifting, and there is an urgent and compelling uprising from all corners of the globe to make sense of it all. What does it mean to be a woman in our rapidly changing world? As societies and institutions question the worth and value of the female species, how do we claim our brilliance and bring forth the positive contribution we know we are here to make? How can we begin to cultivate and strengthen those qualities that elevate not only ourselves but also our communities? And most importantly, how *would* our world be enriched if more women were running the show?

Women Let's Rise is a collection of journeys, insights, and wisdom that invites all of us, male and female, to witness the significant value of having empowered women at the table. Women who know their worth, women who have tapped into their personal values, talents, and strengths, and women who believe that we are here to work together for a greater whole.

In these chapters, you will meet a wide range of women, from those in their twenties to those in their sixties, from educators, designers, sales executives, financial advisors, and event planners to entrepreneurs, coaches, leadership trainers, and spiritual teachers. These women have come from all walks of life to share their unique journeys of leading themselves and leading others through work, business, family, and community. They share their stumbles and their victories on their path to find their voice and use it for the greater good, and they teach us their tips for owning self-confidence, creating human connections, and making an impact. While each woman's story is different, strong themes run through all of them: learning positive self-talk, taking initiative, listening with compassion, building connections, and living with purpose, passion, and vision. Whether you run your little household, the corner office, a mega corporation, or a municipality, these stories will inspire you to show up in bigger ways and use the qualities of patience, encouragement, empathy, unity, and harmony to motivate those around you.

As more women around the globe rise and thrive, mentally, socially, economically, and politically, our turbulent world is being given a new opportunity to shift from division to synergy, competition to collaboration, and egotistical fear to loving kindness.

Many of the women in this book met through FemCity, an international community with online education and local gatherings in over 150 cities to support women in business and in life. Fem-City encourages women to come together and lead through collaboration—something that's also a core value of this collaborative book project and its heart-centered publisher, Golden Brick Road Publishing House (GBR Publishing).

True leadership begins within the heart of every person, regardless of sex or gender; it is not just about making ourselves better but also making those around us better in the process. When more women and feminine qualities run the world, we run for the betterment of all humankind. Join us in this movement to rise, thrive, and lead *with love*.

MIND

THE WILL TO THRIVE

CHAPTER 1

BELIEVE YOU DESERVE SUCCESS

"Show up big for yourself. Imagine if we all loved the way we showed up in the world."

NATALIE ZOMBECK

Natalie Zombeck is a mom, a wife, and an educator to the core. She has been a leader and influencer across various arts disciplines for many years, which made for a natural transition to the classroom twelve years ago. She has always had a love of empowering and connecting with young minds, utilizing her experiences as a musician, dancer, performer, and coach to lift them up and explore their potential both in and out of the classroom walls.

Several years into her teaching career, Natalie was introduced to a new opportunity that allowed her to explore her entrepreneurial spirit; alongside her already full schedule, she built a multi-million dollar business with a global health and wellness company. Fully immersing herself in the paths of both education and business, Natalie has helped men and women of all ages explore their strengths, and tap into their own power to inspire and influence.

nataliezombeck.arbonne.com
ig: natalie.z.nvp | fb: Natalie Zombeck (Comeau)

You feel it, don't you? That little spark of something special in your belly. I know it's there, too. There is a feeling of potential inside that makes you curious. Perhaps ideas float to the surface, only to be followed by "What if . . .?" or "Someday . . ."

When we have a desire to tap into that potential and step into our greatness, sometimes we wonder how it can happen. What can we do when we don't believe we are worthy of our biggest dreams? How can we explore our desires and create a life filled with passion and abundance when doubt and fear keep getting in the way?

I was once there, too, my friend. My vision for my future was always brighter than the reality I was living and creating for myself. But I learned and implemented some fundamental strategies in my own life that allowed me to create the life I once had only wished for. Simple things that shifted my mindset and my perspective and helped me grow my confidence to remove the blocks that were holding me back. You can do the same. A life of abundance is waiting for you to take control and step into your own greatness.

When we were little, we always had an answer ready for the constant question: "What do you want to be when you grow up?" Our answer likely changed over the years as our interests changed, but at some point, most of us had a crazy, outlandish answer like, "I want to be a mermaid princess" or "I want to be a fire truck" or even "I want to live on the moon." Why did we ever think those things were possible? Because back then, we were limitless. We didn't know anything was impossible: we just dreamed. We knew it could happen.

This dreaming mode served us well as we began to think about what we really wanted to be in our adult lives and what we really wanted to do. At some point along the way, though, most of us leave the dreaming mode and enter survival mode. School is done, we are forced into adulthood, and life begins to pile on deadlines, bills, and other responsibilities. The start of adulthood tends to be a time when we forget about those ambitions we once had, the ones we acted out dressed up in the backyard. We put them high up on a shelf with the intention of revisiting them when the time was right, when we had the time and money to do something about them. We trade those dreams in for settling into a life we eventually wish was bigger; then we look back on those big dreams we once had, perhaps peek at them on the shelf, but then decide we can't pursue them anymore. Why does this happen? Why do we lose the courage to try? To stay within the limits around us? To start new things, to take risks, etc? Why do we lose confidence in our once-desired dreams?

There are actually many reasons this can happen: fear, low self-esteem, a solid belief we are not deserving, lack of motivation to do something different, a feeling of unworthiness. These are foundational belief systems that we carry with us through life. They influence our choices and in turn influence the path of our lives. But where do they come from? Very often it's our childhood experiences that shape us and influence us.

I always knew in my heart I was meant for big things. Growing up and into adulthood, I said yes to every opportunity, thinking, Maybe this is it. Maybe this is the thing that's going to lead to my ultimate success.

I was drawn to new things and new experiences. Jumping into every opportunity presented to me meant I was often part of several clubs, choirs, and teams. After I graduated from university I held multiple jobs. Even when I started my career, I had two part-time jobs on the side. I couldn't just sit around and watch life go by without doing everything I could to live it up. The fire in my belly that desired a big life wouldn't let me play small. Maybe it was because of my willingness, my desire to grow and do big things, that I often found myself in leadership roles. I didn't just dance, I taught dance. I didn't just learn to play instruments, I taught the instruments. I didn't take on the typical part-time jobs my friends had as servers or cashiers; rather I was running camps, directing theater productions, and teaching workshops. I had drive, but I also had the inability to channel it into one thing because I had no idea where my path was meant to lead.

Have you ever had the feeling of running but not really getting anywhere?

To some, success is being able to hop on a plane to a beach somewhere at a moment's notice. To others, success means not having to wait to buy blueberries only when they are on sale. Perhaps success means the ability to donate without hesitation to the kids who knock on the door asking for fundraising support. Maybe it means not having a boss or a schedule, or finally acquiring that coveted convertible you've always had an eye on.

I didn't know what success would look like in my life, but I knew what I wanted it to feel like: freedom. Freedom from financial strain, freedom from the nine-to-five, freedom from the obligation to ask for permission to be with a loved one if they got sick or needed me at their side. I knew I had it in me to create that freedom, but here was the problem: ambition can take a back seat when low self-esteem has taken the wheel.

If you struggle with self-doubt, shyness, social awkwardness, fear of commitment, etc., can you pinpoint a time in your life when that first came into play? When something in your past helped to shape your personality? I can. I was twelve.

I blame my ambition. I grew up in a city of 85,000 people, and the kids in my class had gone through school together since kindergarten. When we got to grade seven, two important things happened: I was old enough to be part of the Student Council, and our school was putting on our first ever theater production. Of course I wanted to be part of both! My zest for life, my excitement for all things new and fun was shining bright and I was pumped to participate. I became part of the Student Council and I landed the lead in the play. If you had been in the same room as me during the early days of grade seven, you would have noticed a spring in my step so high I hardly touched the ground. Unfortunately, it didn't last long. This was the year my life changed. My personality changed. My confidence sunk into a plunging downward spiral of sadness, scarcity, and fear.

Isn't it funny how much we allow our self-worth to be defined (influenced) by others? I became a target for bullying, an all too common struggle. The girls in my class became cruel; I hadn't known until that year that people could actually point and laugh at a person. That it didn't just happen in cartoons. They made fun of my clothes, my writing, my laugh; one of them even stole my binder with all of my school work in it for months. No, I promise I didn't lose it; it did, however, magically appear perfectly positioned on top of my desk at the end of the school year, as if it had never left. That year when I earned the opportunity to represent my school at a leadership camp, I was grateful just to be able to leave my classroom for a week.

I will never forget the night I said to my mom, "I don't want to go to school tomorrow." I had said it many times before, as I'm sure most kids do just because they want to sleep in, but this time it was for real. I had developed a debilitating fear of walking into my classroom each day. I would fantasize about clever things I would say next time I was picked on, but in-the-moment wit was not my forte and I usually just walked away, feeling gutted and defeated. I would often make up excuses for why I needed to stay in at recess or ask if I could work somewhere else, away from the taunting. I was grateful for Student Council meetings or play rehearsals because they were my safe place. Thinking back on it, perhaps this is why I studied acting later on; being someone else was easier, and yet, I could shine big in the stage lights like my inner self still craved.

This lack of self-esteem followed me into high school, where I can easily see a pattern emerge, classic of someone suffering from low self-esteem, in my relationships, my fear of being alone, the choices I made . . . Yes, my ambition was still there, but when confidence starts to fade, questions creep in about the possibility of these ambitions happening. If I were to draw a timeline of my life and hang it on the wall, I could take a step back and show you where the results of the bullying resurfaced and affected my life choices later on. "Here," "here," "here": I would show you with my finger on the timeline, and I have no doubt you would say, "Yep, me, too," "Yes, that was me," "I remember that feeling as well." After all, everyone has their things, be it trauma, stress, or loss. Sister, if you are still in that place or are wondering when your life won't be affected anymore, I commend you for taking a step forward by simply picking up this book.

Here's why . . .

My turning-point came from a list of things that I can only describe as lifesavers. I credit my inability to say no to opportunities as the reason I ended up saying yes to starting my own business with a health and wellness company when I was in my mid-twenties. This is where I learned how successful people live, think, and act. These were all new concepts to me, but I immersed myself in learning how I could clear away my head junk and roadblocks and re-discover my confidence and maybe, just maybe, tap into that little spark again. I learned that everyone has stressors, head junk, and hard stuff. But it's how we rise above those things and stand on top of them, rather than being buried beneath them, that ultimately determines where our path will go. I learned that the most important piece to finding success, rising up as a leader, and rediscovering self-worth is our dedication to personal growth. We need to fill our minds with the good stuff, with inspiration from great leaders who will help identify what lights us up and what fills our hearts. By diving into personal growth, we gain perspective, belief in our abilities, and ideas to create the lives we desire.

If this is a foreign concept, I encourage you to open your heart and mind. Daily habits done with intention can create lasting improvements in many areas of our life. My car became my classroom during my daily drives; I listened to inspiring audios, in which the voices of those I wanted to emulate talked me through my head-stuff. I started reading books every day by people who had overcome adversity, learned valuable life lessons, and figured out how to create what they had desired. I ended each day by reading even more. Filling my head with the good stuff helped to re-ignite my fire.

I was also surrounding myself with those who had big visions for their lives and had worked through their own head junk and hard things from the past. They had been able to let go of things holding them back and were living life out loud. I wanted to feel that way again. I needed it. And I learned that it is a choice.

I firmly believe that you are the sum of the five people you spend the most time with. So I recommend taking a good look at who those people are every day. Whose energy is influencing you? Let me tell you, I am proof that surrounding ourselves with people who lift us up, support us, guide us, and cheer us on can give us the strength to repair any damage our souls need to mend. I also chose to do a friend-detox, in which I decided to move on from anyone who was a negative influence in my life, didn't believe in me or my vision, and had nothing to offer but a crappy mindset and lack of support.

At the time, this included the man I was engaged to marry.

Isn't it interesting how we tend to settle for what we think we deserve? I had been stuck, stuck in a relationship that wasn't serving me and was holding me back. I learned later on that my friends and family looked at our relationship with confusion, disbelieving that I would have even chosen this person. We didn't match at all, and my lack of self-worth was to blame. I didn't think I deserved any better.

That low self-worth rut is hard to climb out of when we can't see it any other way. It was starting to show up in other areas of my life, too: my business had stalled, my health wasn't the best, and I wasn't taking great care of myself. I needed something to change. Again. But this time, thanks to the choices I had made with my mindset and growth, instead of descending down a spiral of depression, this time I was on the outside looking in. I saw that I had lowered my standards. I recognized that I wasn't living up to the amazing life I had envisioned for myself; what was worse, while I had made great choices to create a life I wanted, I was self-sabotaging my success by limiting myself in other ways. I wondered why I had allowed the loudest and most influential voice in my life at the time to be someone who was so negative. Someone who didn't have goals. Didn't have ambition. Didn't see value in growth or encourage or support me in a way I should have expected from my partner. My shift came from a combination of personal growth, recognizing the things that held me back, making decisions to rise above them, surrounding myself with the best types of people, and finally clearing away the fog to clearly see the vision I had once wanted for myself.

I knew the only person standing in my way was me. I made a bold decision to change my life circumstances, and I called off our wedding two months before it was to happen. The story itself is quite an epic one that would require a glass of wine and a face-to-face chat cross-legged on my couch. But the moral of the story is: I freed myself from all that was holding me back because I had decided to believe that I deserved success. It can come down to a decision, my friend. But not just a decision to believe it: a decision to act on it, and to make the tough choices because you are worth it.

I had re-ignited a fire in my belly that wasn't going to let anything stop me. Rising above what had only fed doubt and fear was a personal victory that I now see evidence of every. single. day. Since that day, May 5th, 2012, I can proudly point out moments when my bold choice positively influenced my life, and I am forever grateful. Because I raised my bar and made the decision to not settle for less, I have a thriving, growing business that fills me with passion and purpose on a daily basis. I feel healthy. I am now married to my best friend and love of my life; he not only supports and encourages me, he also reminds me daily of my gifts and thanks me for the life we are creating together. I have a beautiful son who will grow up knowing he has the power to create a life without limits. He will watch me set goals and work hard for them. He will watch me fail over and over, but he will always watch me pick myself back up and try again with new focus. He will know the value of a growth mindset and that he really can rise above anything that may challenge him.

When you believe you are worthy of success and can create a life you love, you are able to put into place the things that will help you rise.

Imagine a world where we all love the way we show up. Show up big for yourself. Practice gratitude for every person, lesson, and gift in your day. Be grateful for your vision, the fire in your belly, and embrace each moment that allows you to grow. You deserve it.

CHAPTER 2

CONSIDER THIS

"There is no duplication for the genius and magic of taking persistent action to achieve our goals"

SARAH YEUNG

Sarah Yeung has always dreamed of being a writer. She credits the written word for her ongoing life learning and finds poignancy in language being the only magic that is inexhaustible. Equipped with an intense curiosity for life, she finds brilliance in studying human behavior, history, culture. and the image of "self." As a franchisee owner of 30 Minute Hit in Toronto, Sarah devotes her time to creating an uplifting space for all women to work out, connect and give back to themselves. Sarah maintains a happiness philosophy in which she surrounds herself with good people and finds the time to do the things she loves. She currently lives in Toronto with her two (hefty) cats, Piglet and Dusk, and her partner, Andrew. You'll find her seeking new experiences in the city, cultivating friendships, and always being down to share a laugh.

ig: sarah__yeung | fb: Sarah Yeung

As a kid, I was very critical of my mother for not being a "strong woman."

I could never find the words to define what that bar was; I only detested the hopeless sense of pity I felt when we were sitting across from any form of legal or financial documents. Feeling so incredibly small in the aftermath of my father's sudden heart attack, I made up for it by mentally vying for the position as head of household against the men my mother dated, having somehow developed a pseudo-masculine inferiority complex. I could not wait to grow up and be big enough, smart enough, and strong enough to protect the people I loved.

Where once I was a bubbly grade school kid who played all the school sports and competed with the boys, I developed into a somber and reflective teenager. For years, I sat across from my counselors and thrived in the sickly relish of my own condemnation. I found solace in the online blogosphere, talking to strangers about why I self harmed without ever finding answers. As a young adult, I adopted the mistaken identity of applying to older men and exploiting my sexuality as an avenue to feminine prowess. I became very adept in covering up the underlying belief that I was undeserving of success while exemplifying outward accomplishments. This first appeared at the end of high school when I was connected to a network marketing company and was introduced to mentorship for the first time. I felt the power of belief when someone made you feel special and potentially worthy. Within a year, I built a small team and poured myself into books recommended with the intent to absorb as many success principles as possible.

I moved out of my family home, quit social media, lost my high school friends and landed myself a $40k salary job at eighteen.

However skilled I was in posing as a person of means, my self image at the time reflected a deep rooted disdain for my existence which revealed itself when I ultimately fell out of touch with my mentors. Having made the decision to not attend post-secondary school, I was in a rut to prove myself capable by other means, which led me to my move, three years later, from Vancouver to Toronto where I became co-owners with my sister to the first 30 Minute Hit location in the city.

In subscribing to the principles I continue to read and re-read, I have found in them guidance through my struggles with entrepreneurship, setting boundaries, and building a healthy self-dialogue to continue my ongoing adult education. For all of us today who feel stymied by the overwhelming speed of our interactions or weighed down by the constant pressure to be "productive," here's to a better understanding of ourselves, grounded in science and experience, to effect success and joy in our lives.

One of my favorite success books is *Psycho-Cybernetics* by Maxwell Maltz. Maltz introduced me to the idea that the human mind-body connection is similar to mechanical cybernetics. This scientific perspective helps explain how to best utilize our natural servo-mechanism (our bodies) for success by directing our innate 'machine" to fulfill our innermost image of "self" (our minds). In other words, the study of self-image.

Maltz explains that our internal visualization of goals has a direct connection to what we can achieve on the outside. As with mechanical cybernetics, the body (machine) will only function to perform what is visualized by the head (us). However, once a goal is selected and consciously engaged, we have to learn to *let go* in order for our automatic mechanisms to fulfill their creative function. After all, it's hard to thread a needle when you try too hard. Maltz further finds that a person's inner attitudes will always set the benchmark for their outer success. And science shows that our central nervous system *cannot* differentiate between a detailed, imagined experience versus reality. Since reality is as we perceive with our five senses, our natural mechanism (body) will react, *as if*, to the reality our minds decides to be true. In other words, our outer success will never rise above what we can visualize inside.

To summarize, what I came to understand was this: we make up our own realities.

I became obsessed with this concept. The fact that we can *think* ourselves to greater success than we know captivated me then, and it captivates me still.

My reality as a young girl was stained with the effects of feeling inept - precisely because I am a girl, because I am too young, and because I do not know any better. It is a mad inception game to change our own realities, particularly ones ingrained from our childhoods, but in continuously subscribing to a healthier, happier version of myself, it has become my truth today.

I am thankful to be included in this book of women who thrive through empowerment and leadership. There is no better time to reflect on our collective strength because we are women, because we are the future and because we learn through one another.

THE KEY WORD IS: GO!

Dan Ariely, a professor of Psychology and Behavioural Economics at Duke University, engages in some of my favorite studies of human behavior and motivation. One of his experiments that deeply resonated with me is the "door game." In this computer game, he allotted student players one hundred clicks to look for money, being paid out in real cash bonuses, behind three virtual doors. The rules were simple: players clicked to enter a door, and each subsequent click inside that door earned a little money, with the sum varying each time. Players could switch through doors to find the highest payout; logic suggests that once the players found the largest payout, they would stay there and cash out.

To add to the game, each door that was un-clicked would slowly shrink and eventually disappear. This visual stimulus ended up costing the students a fifteen percent decrease in their pay, by "wasting" their clicks trying to keep all the doors open. When the cash fee stimulus was introduced to keep the doors open, students ended up losing money! Even a version that allowed students to re-open disappeared doors at no cost produced the same result.

What did this controlled experiment show? The troubling irrationality of our current society plagued by indecision because of *too many* choices. In the anxiety we feel towards the unknown, or the potential for another future, it results in the inhibition of our own success.

At the age of twenty-one, I put this experiment into application.

When the opportunity arose to open the first flagship 30 Minute Hit location in Toronto, I felt both thrilled and stunned by the proposal. I was cushy in my safe job, accumulating savings, happy with my apartment and my two cats . . . all in all, my life was good. Did I want to mess that up? Uproot my comfortable Vancouver life and move to Toronto, where I had no connections, no friends, and certainly no business background?

Yes.

I drew inspiration from my old boss who owned her location in Vancouver for the dream lifestyle as a business owner. I saw the ability to foster and create a community of women I would grow to love. I imagined my team of trainers and how I would learn to best serve them and improve myself as a leader.

In visualizing the goal, I was less concerned about the money or whether this was a good bet against the odds. Without any undue unrest about making the "right" decision, I simply went ahead to see what would happen. And funnily enough, the doors opened.

As with all memorable life experiences, I failed spectacularly in my first year. Even into my second year, I continue to be enlightened on a daily basis as to what it means to be a business owner. As much as I had built my mindset, there is no duplication for the genius and magic of taking persistent action to achieve our goals. More than moving and opening the business, being present and finding reward in daily operations was where I grew the most. Just as a machine functions to its true purpose through problem solving, so do we too feel the satisfaction of progress in first selecting our obstacles, and then solving them. Bearing in mind that even the most advanced machine solves only one problem at a time, in direct contrast to our cultural disposition to "multitask" as the only means of being successful. To try and force production by overfeeding any mechanism will only ever result in one code: error.

In reflection of my initial decision to move, had I remained stumped by the myriads of colorful doorways available, I wouldn't be here today. So when next presented with an opportunity (or problem), remember to apply to that genius imagination within us, that which helps us interpret and build our concept of realities, and realize that our possibilities and answers to them are boundless and can be re-imagined into new scenarios. Selecting one course of action lends to the absolute peace of deciding to act. Matter of fact, focus on building that one empire, and look out for other doorways to open up.

So pick a doorway, and in you go.

TROUBLESHOOTING: MORE THAN ONE WAY

More than ever, we have options today.

While we might get caught up in the preliminary rounds for *what* to pursue, the tangents *while* in pursuit are equally testing.

One of the most awkward and painful realizations I had in my earliest days of entrepreneurship was that my sister and I were not well suited for one another in our business partnership.

This realization caused me a massive amount of conflicted guilt and bitterness. When the idea to separate was proposed, it created a rift between us on a personal and professional level. I feared losing a sisterly relationship, but I was also frustrated at feeling "stuck" in a partnership that was not progressing.

Was I being selfish/unfair/wrong for making this call? How do you measure those factors against your own happiness and success?

As Maltz said in regard to our inner servo-mechanism, we react to the reality we perceive to be true. Dwelling on the feeling of being stuck caused me to see only one of two ways: If I/she gets what she/I want, how do I/she get what she/I want?

There's much to be said about our individual perception of reality. Fully understanding and applying this concept to the people around us, especially towards people who think differently than us, can provide the insight we need to begin new levels of acceptance.

With all the disagreements I felt with my sister as a business partner, it seemed too easy and magical that those same feelings could dissipate after submitting to the imagination of her reality. Seeing her inner mechanism fulfill its role in reacting to her truth, though at odds with mine, took my perceived slight out of the equation entirely. And without this injured prejudice, we could engage new conversation as to how we could both achieve our goals individually without taking away from one another in the process.

Of all my lessons in discovering human nature, this one has by far provided me with the most sense of contentment and peace. Whether we dwell on our own faults or on the faults of others, such judgment does not align with the progression of our goal-oriented inner mechanisms. Much like we should not forcefully remember all of our previous failures while we develop a new skill, we cannot expect to see new realities while holding onto a negative one.

Forgiving ourselves and others of a negative reality can result in the dramatic improvement in our ability to live our lives in much better harmony, in more ways than we once thought possible.

UNEXPECTED REALITIES

Having announced my decision to separate ownership, I was on the cusp of moving to open my own location in North York, when a decision was forced upon the business to relocate. Fast.

Unable to secure a new lease in time, I experienced the closure of my first ever business venture.

All experiences in life are ultimately enriching. Nothing so far in my life has broken my heart in quite the same way as the closure of my business, but nothing has also come close to the incredible realization of what I had built. Coming away with an incredible team of trainers, our closure further highlighted the sincerest loyalty and friendships made within our community of women who were touched by a passion project turned vocation, eager to rejoin us again. On our last day, we all toasted and celebrated together.

Despite these successes, I suffered with thoughts of incompetence as a business owner, owing guilt to my perceived failure to continue serving my team and my community, stuck on my recurring inability to protect anyone from any perceived threat or discomfort, once more . . . My generation, often dubbed "snowflakes," are often too readily discouraged and derailed by the simple cycle of negative feedback in life. There are some invariable laws in our world that no matter what we subscribe to in our faiths, appear to test and challenge us in order to grow. We can call it blessings in disguise, necessary evils or tough love.

In Maltz's understanding, our auto mechanism *only* learns through negative feedback. When we mispronounce a few words, we don't conclude that we shouldn't be speaking the language at all. Developing a healthy relationship with negative feedback is learning the ability to adjust accordingly and to *forget* the incorrect attempt in favor of the successful one. Provided that we learn to accept inevitable negative feedback in informative ways, we are best on track to uncover new means of success. Grounded in the understanding of this necessary learning curve in life allowed me to reset my goals and find my way back to being a business owner again.

While this episode in my life has been arguably one of the toughest so far, it has also been the most fruitful. Having spent most of my early life combating what I interpreted as acquiescent in my mother's response to a tragedy, I learned that being strong-willed and assuming the stance of a "strong, independent business woman" does not eclipse having grace when things don't turn out the way we planned. The world is sometimes a harder place than you thought it to be, but if you mentally adjust to accept the challenge, it's got to be onwards and upwards.

WHAT I KNOW NOW

I think a lot now about what I meant by my criticism of my mother. I would like to think I have learned something more about being a strong woman since the time I judged her so severely. From a previously spoiled and inert eleven-year-old girl, who first discovered the power of introspection within the four walls of her counsellor's office, I now recognize the unfair and self-righteous ideology of a "strong woman" that I had imposed on my mom.

In this hotly debated topic, a strong woman can be coined as being outspoken, brave, and decisive. True. Yet there are equally as many examples of strong female characters who contribute and lead through their gentle nature, feminine instinct, and graceful guidance. Also true.

My personal experiences thus far have shown me the benefit of being flexible on my definition of the term. The term is in equal parts situational, circumstantial, and sentimental. The best guideline I've found is through the continuing study and application towards our best selves, learning by reading, subscribing to the ethos of making our own (positive) realities, and to the best of my ability, living a fearless life of giving first in return for greater joy and success.

CHAPTER 3

MIRROR, MIRROR

"It's time to become more aware of the power we have within ourselves, and it all begins with what we see in the mirror."

PAMELA D'IPPOLITO

Pamela D'Ippolito's life may seem like a series of ups and downs. While she has often been considered "lucky," she has also faced great adversity, including a crippling medical diagnosis that was reversed after fifteen years. It wasn't until the recent death of her youngest daughter that Pamela really understood how important mindset would be in moving forward with her life. She chose to be mentored directly by Bob Proctor, world renowned expert in human potential, and realized that we don't have to be victims to the world around us. Pamela now devotes her time to studying and understanding the power within. As a Certified Proctor Gallagher Consultant and Mindset Strategist, Pamela helps others realize the importance of self-image, gratitude, and mindset. She is committed to helping people gain strength amongst their chaos, turn their thinking into results, and live their best possible lives.

www.h2b2strategies.com
ig: @this.is.me.pam.d | fb: @pamvarma

When I was growing up, I never realized the extent to which my mind was a sponge. I was a permanently intrigued child, always absorbing. Reading was my passion, and I would devour books so quickly that we would often make daily trips to the library. I don't think I was alone: it's safe to say that all children are sponges. Eager, willing, hopeful, listening to all that is around them. In fact, the environment in which we are raised has more of an effect on us as individuals than heredity does.

When we are born, we are complete blank slates. Yes, we have certain traits that have been passed down via DNA, but everything else is learned. The fact that I love a good Quebecois poutine, squeaky cheese and all, isn't because I am half French Canadian and it's in my genes. It's because it is a dish I saw my family love from a young age. Likewise, being bilingual wasn't written into my DNA; I was simply exposed to both English and French on a daily basis. Our food preferences, spoken languages, reactions to certain stimuli (like seeing a spider), beliefs about the world, beliefs about *ourselves* are all learned. When we are repeatedly exposed to something that triggers an emotion (a certain food makes us happy, a spider frightens us), it imprints onto our subconscious mind (considered the emotional mind). While the conscious mind (the intellectual or educated mind) has the ability to reject a notion ("No, the sky is not green, it is blue!"), the subconscious mind cannot. As a result, how we grow and develop, and more importantly, *who* we grow and develop into, is primarily based on the beliefs, habits, and behaviors we learn and embed into our subconscious minds without even realizing it. The groupings of these habitual subconscious beliefs and behaviors are called paradigms. Paradigms control our thoughts, which control our actions, which control our results in life. More specifically, our personal paradigms (the group of habitual thoughts and behaviors we have about ourselves) will determine how we see our role and purpose in this world. They will determine whether we are the lead character in our own movie or just "lady on bus" in the credits.

I think it's safe to say that we all want to be the Oscar-winning actress in our life story, but often we feel more like an extra. So how do we change that? First, we need to be aware of the different ingrained thoughts we have in order to recognize how they are truly affecting our lives. Typically, paradigms will fall into three categories: neutral, positive, and negative. Let's break it down; it's not as complicated as it seems, but it is life-changing!

NEUTRAL

I don't think my ingrained love of poutine is harmful to anything other than my GI tract; therefore I can classify it as neutral. Language spoken, food devoured, the way you put your toilet paper roll on the holder (a hot topic, I know!) are all pretty neutral learned behaviors. As long as we remain open to each others' ways and do not judge, there is no harm to self or others in these types of paradigms.

POSITIVE

Ever meet a family that is almost exclusively made up of math geniuses? Guess what probably happened in that household? At some point, a grandparent said, "Oh, numbers run through our blood! We are human abacuses!" This belief then ingrained on the parent, who grew up believing, "Wow, numbers run through our blood! We are human calculators!", which then ingrained on their children. Truth is, math skills are not carried through DNA. As babies, each individual in that math-gifted family had roughly the same potential in math brain power as most other babies around the world. The difference is that their soft baby brains were imprinted with the notion of mathematics mastery, and they deemed it to be true. Remember, the subconscious mind cannot reject what is imprinted on it; it must accept. And so as this notion has been reinforced into the subconscious mind, the individual believes it to be true because they have repeatedly been told it, and so it is. Just as a baby in an English-speaking household learns English without missing a beat, a baby in a math genius household would believe they also are a math wiz and would sail through working with numbers.

I grew up in a household that firmly believed in the importance of academics. This imprinting started when I was a wee child. What do you think the outcome was? I think grades above ninety-six percent in all advanced level math and science courses in high school and beyond speak for themselves. I was constantly told that these subjects were my strength and focus and that they came easily to me. And so they did. I did not slave over textbooks every night. Yes, I did my homework and showed up to class. But did I study for hours before a test? No. Did I pull all-nighters memorizing formulas? Nope. I honestly just wholeheartedly, one hundred percent believed that I was a naturally smart individual. Not cocky, just confident. And as I deemed it to be true, so it was.

I'm putting all this into the positive category because being told you're good at something feels good. Believing you are a success feels good. It creates confidence and boosts self-worth. Praise, specifically directed at *you*, feels good. And so these types of paradigms have an overall positive effect on our lives.

NEGATIVE

Now this is where it can all go downhill. As the subconscious mind cannot reject, imagine its exposure to negativity. Just as some children grow up believing they are math geniuses, others are instead told, "Our family sucks at math" or "Money doesn't grow on trees" so they'll always have to work hard for it. Again, just as language is learned and ingrained, so are beliefs about intellect, success, and destiny.

One day when I was twenty-two years old, I randomly fainted. I went to the doctor, as suggested. They ran tests and I was diagnosed with a specific type of muscular dystrophy. At the time, other than the fainting (which actually is not a symptom of muscular dystrophy), I had given absolutely no indication of having the condition. None. I could run and take the stairs two at a time, all while wearing sky-high stiletto shoes. But as is customary with a new diagnosis, the medical team took the time to explain how it would impact my life, including everything I would *not* be able to do. I was informed I would eventually no longer be able to raise my arms above my head, I would no longer be able to navigate stairs unassisted, I may eventually be unable to walk!

What do you think happened? Within a few years, I was no longer able to run, jump, or get up a set of stairs unassisted. I definitely could no longer wear my beloved heels. Most of what was predicted, dictated, imprinted onto me came true. But should it have?

WHAT ARE YOU SAYING TO YOURSELF?

Go stand in front of the mirror. What are the thoughts that instantly run through your head?

"I look frumpy and tired."

"I have rolls like the Pillsbury Doughboy."

"I suck at public speaking."

"I have zero creativity."

"I always date losers."

"I suck with money. I'm always broke."

"Nothing good ever happens to me."

Does any of this sound familiar? If yes, then STOP IT!

Think about what we are doing to ourselves! All of these phrases and thoughts trigger emotions, which go straight to where? Our subconscious (emotional) minds that cannot reject what we are telling them! In thinking these self-limiting thoughts about ourselves, we are actually accepting them as truth, and as a result, they become our reality. Of course you are not a good public speaker: you just decided you weren't, so you are proving it to be true. You're right, you don't have any creative ideas because you've decided you don't, so you shut down any possibility of thinking some up.

A few months ago, I received a phone call from my specialist, fifteen years after my initial diagnosis. They had gotten it wrong. I did not, in fact, have the type of muscular dystrophy with which I had been labelled. To say I was shocked is an understatement. Now, as a mindset strategist, I understand how damaging this initial label, or more specifically the conditions attached to it, has been. I understand how this imprinted on me and became a self-fulfilling prophecy. I had had absolutely no indications of illness, but they magically started appearing when I was told they would . . . for a specific condition I did not end up having.

Do I actually have a neuromuscular condition? Yes, probably. Is there a high likelihood that I was so distraught by this diagnosis, so open and raw, that whatever I was told to expect infiltrated every cell in my body? Yes. Could any of my afflictions have been exacerbated because I believed them to be the final destination of my health? Definitely.

Take another look in the mirror, but this time picture your four-year-old self. Wide-eyed, hopeful, excited to discover the world. Now imagine, just as you are teaching your four-year-old self how to write her name, you are also teaching her to hate herself. You are teaching her that she has no value in her future career, that she shouldn't be happy with her physical appearance, that she will not be capable of holding genuine relationships. That she will suck at life. How does that make you feel? Should we *ever* say that to a four-year-old? The answer is a definite NO! Why then do we feel it is okay to say it to ourselves now? To embed these debilitating thoughts into our subconscious minds? How can we expect to excel in life when we are simultaneously squashing our self-worth?

As women, we have been taught to be modest, to diminish ourselves so as to not seem too bold, to be happy with what we are given yet not be happy with our bodies, to be a supporting player for others, to not ask for help but not be too independent . . . it's confusing and out of touch and is creating crippling paradigms that literally make the difference between immobility and rising to the occasion.

MIRROR WORK

So how do you change the negative paradigms that have been created, the ones that are preventing you from stepping into your greatness? You do a little mirror work.

Since your limiting paradigms were created by repeatedly imprinting negative thoughts onto your subconscious mind, those paradigms have to be changed the same way: continuous repetition of the new thought. There is no more effective way to ingrain a new belief than by facing yourself each and every day and telling yourself these new truths. If we can look ourselves in the mirror, say that our butt is too flat, and believe it, then we can also look at ourselves in the mirror and instead say that we are proud of our healthy bodies. Eventually, we will believe that instead.

Here are some steps to help you break down and replace your current paradigms.

1. Think of yourself. Write down all that comes to mind, in all aspects of your life. Make this a mind purge, writing down all the words that flow through the pen to the paper. Spend a good twenty minutes on this.

2. Have a look at what you've written. Highlight those positive thoughts, the ones that make you feel good. Your cheeks have a natural glow? Circle that! You bake the most delicious cookies on the planet? Highlight that! You have won numerous career awards for your expert coding? Gold star beside that one! Now transfer all of those positive attributes to a new piece of paper.

3. Go back to your mind purge page. What are the negative stories you are telling yourself? Re-write those on a different piece of paper.

4. For each negative story, re-write the opposite on the positive page. So for example, if you wrote, "I am always broke,"
the opposite would be, "I am a money master! It flows to
me with ease on a continuous basis." If you wrote, "I eat
like garbage," the opposite would be, "I enjoy nutritious
food in sufficient quantities to fuel my body." The key is to
rewrite the story using positive words in the present tense.
Do this for every single negative story that you have written
down, and for any that may come up during the process.

5. Take your sheet with the negative stories and burn it. Yes,
you read that correctly: *burn it*. Safely, of course! As you
destroy this sheet of paper, close your eyes and imagine
yourself purging these thoughts from your mind. This act is
symbolic but has great power in breaking down the limiting
paradigms in your subconscious mind. They need to be de-
stroyed, and that is what we are doing!

6. Close your eyes and envision your dream day, a day when
everything in your life is exactly as you've wished. Perhaps
you finally had the courage to apply for that huge promotion and you got it! Perhaps you are the CEO of your own
successful company. Perhaps you are just owning your life
in all aspects. It doesn't matter if you want to run a business
but have no clue what type. Allow your mind to run wild, independent of your current situation. What are you wearing
on this dream day? Where are you and with whom? Try to
piece out every single detail to the best of your ability. Now
write it down. Always written in the present tense (as if it is
already happening—"I AM a successful, world-renowned
baker!") and in the positive ("I live in financial abundance"
as opposed to "I don't have debt."). Let the creativity flow.
Dream big. Write it like the storyline of your life's movie,
only this time, you are the Oscar-winning lead actress.

7. You now have two sheets of paper: one filled with your positive traits, including those that are yet to come to fruition,
and your life script. Now comes the mirror work. Every day,
in the morning and at night, you are going to look at your-

self in the mirror and read your positive traits, out loud, to yourself. Then you are going to read your life story, out loud, to yourself. Morning and night. Every. Single. Day.

It may seem excessive. Initially it will be embarrassing, awkward; you'll want to avoid it like the plague. But remember, our original paradigms were created through constant repetition. The same must be done to replace them. Think of it like a muscle. If you were to wrap your left arm in a sling and only ever use your right arm, eventually your left arm would atrophy and the right arm would become super strong. The same goes for paradigms. You are wrapping up your negative stories (burning them, symbolically releasing them) and focusing on your new positive truths. Soon, with constant repetition, the new positive truths will become stronger and take over.

It won't be quick and it won't be easy. It took fifteen years of daily reminders of my limitations to get to my current degree of physical weakness. I can't expect to reverse it all in three days. In fact, based on the level of "damage" that has been done, I need help. I have hired personal trainers and committed to nutrition that will fuel my body, all on top of the mirror work. I've decided that I don't need another label to tell me what I will not be able to achieve. I don't have to wait until the doctors figure it out before stepping in to my best self. I can start now, take charge of my own health and my own success, and become the leader of my own life.

Trust me when I say the work will be worth it. You won't believe yourself at first, but just picture that four-year-old self. Wide-eyed, absorbing every single word. With commitment and dedication to the process, you'll become less skeptical. You'll start to feel better. You'll notice yourself stepping into your truth and rising into your own self-leadership, the main actor in your life movie. Eventually you'll believe it all. And one day, when you look at your mirror on the wall and ask "Who is strong, fierce, and can win above all?" the answer will be you. And you'll know it's true.

CHAPTER 4

BELIEF: THE KEY TO CREATING A LIFE YOU LOVE

"Be bold. Be brave. Be disruptive. You are capable of things far beyond your wildest dreams if you just have the courage to go for it."

CHRISTINA WHITELEY

Growing up in a small town on the west coast of BC, Christina experienced challenges after being bullied through her school years. As she overcame the effects of bullying, Christina developed a passion for empowering women and helping them find their own voice.

Christina was a successful hairstylist who owned and operated a salon and on-site wedding business. But she yearned to make a bigger impact than the hair industry could offer and began looking for an opportunity to empower, instill confidence, and provide insight. Four years ago, she realized that she could make a bigger impact and empower more people to live up to their full potential, think outside the box, and start living the life of their dreams.

Now a social media guru and lifestyle influencer, Christina helps women turn their mess into a message and boost their business through social media. She and her husband, Ryan, are stay-at-home parents to their four-year-old daughter, Isabella. They sold their house in the city and live on their dream acreage in the country and are committed to building their family legacy together.

Christina continues to use her influence through public speaking, content marketing, and social media to motivate women who want to take control of their lives and start living with purpose to stand for something bigger than themselves. She strives to empower women to follow their passion and live a life that will inspire those around them.

www.christinawhiteley.com
ig: @thechristinawhiteley | fb: @christina.whiteley.54
li: @/christinawhiteley | t: @christina_lucia
Tiktok: @thechristinawhiteley

How does one come to live the life of their dreams? The truth is, it doesn't happen overnight, but it can happen more quickly than you think if you're ready to take action and work for it.

First, you need to get crystal clear about what you want. If money and time freedom were not a factor, what would you want your life to look like? Would you want to live in the city or out in the mountains? Spend time at the beach or in a foreign country? What would you spend your time doing? Making memories with your family? Reading books? Learning another language? Experiencing different cultures around the world? Crafting a business plan or developing an idea?

I want you to come up with as many details of your dream life as possible and write them down. Then I want you to write out *why* you want this life—what it will mean to you when you have it. You can't take action if you don't know exactly where you are going, because a wish is a dream without a plan.

You can also do this fun exercise with your family. Ask your partner on date night or your kids around the dinner table what they would spend their time doing if they could do anything they wanted every day of the week.

If you're already rolling your eyes, then I've lost you. You can go back to living the same old life, the same way you have been for years. Because let's face it, you're not ready. This chapter is only for those of you who have the desire to step into your full potential and are ready to do what it takes to get there. So stop, right now, go get a pen and paper, and do this activity with me, because if you don't do it now, then you probably won't do it at all. If you are ready to rise above wherever you are right now in your life, I want you to physically write out your goals. I want you to hold these goals and dreams close to your heart and put them somewhere that you will see daily. Maybe it's your closet or bathroom mirror; I prefer the fridge so that whenever I'm bored and want a snack, I'm reminded of what goals I have and where to refocus my energy.

Next, I want you to think about the crew of people you spend the most time with: this is your circle of influence. It could be your co-workers, friends, family, and spouse. Are these people helping or hindering you when it comes to living a life you're in love with? Do they cheer you on? Do they support and encourage you? Do they push you to keep going when things get tough? Are they more successful than you? Do you look up to them? Can you learn from their experience or expertise? If you answered "no" to the majority of these questions, it's time to change things up. You cannot go after greatness if you are not willing to level up. The people you spend the most time with will determine your success. Do not allow people who have settled or given up on their dreams make you question your own. If you wouldn't trade places with them, don't heed their advice.

Attempt to get in front of people you want to be like or want to learn from. Go to events with these people, ask questions, and listen. Some of the most valuable information I have ever received was delivered for free at Q&A's with guest speakers, authors at book signings, speakers at conferences, influencers at networking events, or through conversations and sharing ideas around the dinner table afterward.

Next you need to become a problem solver. Instead of looking for jobs that will diminish your time freedom and more than likely not pay you enough, search for better opportunities. If you see something you're interested in, ask questions. My life wouldn't be as abundant as it is now if I didn't have the courage to pivot from my job as a hairstylist to find a career more aligned with spending time with family and fulfilling my purpose by empowering other women to have a voice and make an impact.

We have free education literally at our fingertips through podcasts, online courses, Youtube, and platforms like TED Talks. Don't take this for granted! People don't want to learn by sitting in a classroom anymore; they want to learn from people who have gained success from being out there in the world, making things happen. There is infinite information available to you at any time of day, so having "no time to learn" is really no excuse. Make time. This is your life we are talking about here. You can learn *anything* you want from the comfort of your home while staying in your pajamas.

Many of us grew up with self-limiting beliefs placed on us by family members when we were very young. You might not even recognize these beliefs because they are so deeply embedded in who you believe you are. But if you think you have to put everyone else before yourself, it may start there. Maybe they told you that your dreams were just "dreams." Maybe they told you that you should be more practical and focus on a formal education so you can take care of yourself if, god forbid, you don't find a man to do that for you (heavy sarcasm with an eye roll here).

I myself was constantly bullied by a group of girls from grade four until I graduated high school. They made fun of me, and I felt shameful of any relationship I was ever in because I felt unworthy and undeserving of being loved. Girls who were jealous called me a homewrecker and a slut for crushing on a popular guy who seemed to take a liking to me but who also lied to me and said he was single. They pushed me into lockers in the halls, and in a few instances I feared for my life. I wonder if those girls will ever read this and realize how cruel and unjustified their actions were—wishful thinking, I guess.

I always tried to operate with kindness and integrity, but as I've come to learn from years of therapy, a fifteen-year-old brain doesn't make great decisions all the time; at that age, your brain isn't fully developed. Sometimes my decisions left me vulnerable to more ridicule. I spent decades beating myself up for things I wish I could have done differently to avoid being hurtfully gossiped about by those bullies. The confidence I carry today comes from years of therapy and personal development, and by becoming a woman who isn't always perfect but one who I am proud of.

The biggest challenge of all in overcoming your limiting beliefs will be your mindset. You tell yourself: I'm just a small town girl, just a college drop-out, just a wife, just a mom, I've never really succeeded at anything. But this is not the truth. You are exactly who you *decide* to be.

I decided to become obsessed with personal growth and grew into a personal development junkie. I listen to audiobooks and podcasts on leadership and overcoming obstacles. I filled my soul with daily inspiration so that when things go sideways—and yes, they sometimes still do—I have solid habits with which to override the fear and find strength. Yes, you may need to learn a few new skills, sacrifice some sleep or some time watching TV, but a few years of small sacrifice can lead to a lifetime of freedom and memories with the people you love most, instead of working at an uninspiring job.

Now that you know that your thoughts create your reality, you are learning to be resourceful, and you have a clear picture of where you are going, it's time to take action. But first, I want to talk to you a little bit about some of the roadblocks you will face, especially as a woman. Life isn't fair, and you won't be the exception to this rule. When people say to me, "Wow! You're so lucky to have found the success you've had in your industry, you're so motivated and inspiring," I literally want to scream. You think "luck" got me here? Hardly. I have lost jobs because my female manager felt threatened by my drive and ambition. My friends started to avoid me because they thought I was crazy to leave my successful career as a hairstylist and enter into what they perceived as a battleground of judgment and social ridicule. I've also been forced to work in environments in which I have been harassed, sexually assaulted, and verbally abused. I once lost a bartending job that I needed to pay rent because, and I quote, "You don't have enough fun at work. You're focused now on healthy living and there are younger girls [I was twenty-seven] who would kill for your job, to drink and party and flirt with patrons every weekend. You're in a relationship now and quite frankly, you're not as fun." I, of course, disagreed, but I walked away without making a fuss because my boyfriend, now husband, was also an employee of the establishment and I didn't want to risk us both being out of a job at the same time. It literally crushed my soul when I realized I was getting fired for not drinking *enough* on the job.

Another important realization I had is that as a working woman, you don't have the same opportunities as a man *because* you can bear children. Employers know that most of us, at some point, will take maternity leave, and we will also be responsible for care on sick days or if our child or spouse is injured. Employers continue to promote men over women, to high-paying positions most of the time.[1] That's why I'm so obsessed with the online industry, entrepreneurship, and the home business model. No glass ceiling, no one to tell me how much I can or can't make: I decide.

But again, nothing is ever perfect. My team is ninety-five percent women and where there are women, there are egos, jealousy, gossip, and different styles of communication. You basically need to become bulletproof to overcome the emotional rollercoaster of leading a team of women. You have to learn how to communicate with people you don't get along with, you have to learn how to navigate negativity and deflect it as opposed to absorbing it. You also must learn how to create boundaries and make decisions that not everyone is going to approve of. As a retired "people pleaser," my biggest accomplishment, and one that allowed me the most growth, was getting over the fact that not everyone is going to like me, and that is okay. You must commit to growing in your leadership role daily, which in turn creates growth in your business. It all just falls into place when you decide that you're not willing to stay where you are but instead are willing to fight for what you want and need.

There will be moments of doubt, I promise you. You will be emotionally drained and tired and you will think, "What if I can't do this? Then what?" This moment is the exact point when you are at forty percent capacity in terms of your commitment to personal growth and living up to your full potential— this is actually the tipping point that separates those who *do* from those who *wish they could*, and those who quit here end up living out the rest of

---

1   Catalyst. (2019, August 7). Women in management: Quick take. Retrieved from https://www.catalyst.org/research/women-in-management/

their days without ever having the life they truly desire. I urge you, on days like this, to do some self-care: go to the spa, lose yourself in your favorite book, take yourself for lunch at your favorite restaurant and catch a matinee by yourself so you can eat all the popcorn, call a girlfriend who supports you, or hit a yoga class and meditate. Throw the day in the fuck-it bucket, do some self-reflection and journalling, and start again the next morning. Those days are my moments of clarity, when I realize that I still remember the days when I dreamed of the life I'm living right now.

Life isn't perfect, nothing ever is, so you have to look for the silver lining in every circumstance and find joy in the little things. You *have* to celebrate your wins, no matter how big or small, and relish in your accomplishments, because the world is quick to quiet you through judgement and jealousy. You simply have to rise above to be the most powerful and successful version of yourself.

I exchanged two years of binge-watching Netflix after I put my daughter to bed each night for a self-taught crash course on social media and online marketing, which in turn helps our family bring in a quarter million dollars a year, and rising. We live in our dream home on acreage in the country where my husband has just started developing the land to start a business and create our estate legacy. We have dreams of a family cottage on the lake, and our daughter started preschool at a private school this year. None of this would have been possible on a bartender and hairstylist income.

You have the ability to make quantum leaps in your life, but you have to learn that working harder isn't always the answer; sometimes you just have to pivot. How people make money is changing, society is changing. There is a huge world out there waiting for you, and you just need the courage to take one small step every day toward your goal. I've learned that you don't have to know everything, but you *can* learn anything. It may not happen on your expected timeline, but if you take quitting off the table, inevitably the "how" shows up when you least expect it.

The key to it all is daily gratitude for what you *do* have. The day-to-day things we take for granted are often those we miss when reflecting back on our lives. I learned this trick from a friend:

every morning I go on a one minute "gratitude rant" in which I speak out loud the things I am grateful for. This sets the tone for my entire day. It goes something like this . . .

"I'm grateful that I'm breathing and healthy. I live in my dream home where I wake up and hear the birds singing or the rain falling on the roof. We have a wood stove to keep us warm, we have high-quality, organic food to fuel our health, we have good friends and a kind family. I love the women I work with and radiate happiness for their growth and accomplishments. I have a husband who loves me and a brilliant daughter who has my heart. I love our dogs and our freedom to design each day the way we want. I am so grateful we get to live this life and help others find their freedom, too."

I've spent fifteen years doing personal development, getting over past trauma, and growing into the woman I am today. And the truth is, I'm still not even close to living up to my full potential. I've learned that success isn't about money: it's about getting what you want out of life and doing the things you love, with the people you care about most. I've learned that life happens in chapters and that each one, good or bad, has a lesson attached. But ultimately, we get to write our own ending.

Don't ever forget that your daily choices, or lack of choice, create your reality.

If any of this is speaking to you, I encourage you to reach out to me. I would love to hear your goals and dreams and help you express your voice. Let's turn your mess into a message and use it to inspire and help others. I want to help you take action and come up with a plan so you, too, can start living a life you don't need a vacation from. This is your chance. Your time is now.

CHAPTER 5

THE DOMINO EFFECT

"Master your mind, and everything else will begin to realign itself."

ANNIE NGU

Annie Ngu is a multi-passionate leader who has been featured in Girlboss, the online community platform for women, and in *The Women Wave*. She has written for *Elite Daily*, *Narcity Toronto*, *Prototypr*, and *For Working Ladies*, among other publications including her own *OFFtheRECORD*. Best known for her work as co-founder of the Women United Project, Annie is making her debut into the world of authorship in *Women Let's Rise*.

Annie is a role model for women in design, as well as for women everywhere. Her goal is to empower women to be resilient, live well, and love with the utmost self-respect. Her focus with the Women United Project is to create a culture of inclusivity and love within ourselves and the world by mastering our minds.

https://anniengu.com
ig: @anguphoto | li: @anniengu
t: @AnnieNgu | Goodreads: @anniengu

I'm Annie. I'm a creative individual who lives with anxiety.

On good days, my mind is my greatest ally. On other days, it can be my enemy. It's a constant battle between how I feel and what I think. It has taken a lot of practice to be patient with myself, give space for the negative thoughts to leave one by one, and to remind myself that I am enough despite whatever it is I'm feeling or thinking.

My desire to live worry-free with abundance, gratitude, and purpose meant that some things had to change. For me, that change kept showing up as the need to master my mind in order to be free and live authentically as possible. So I put myself into the growth mindset to #GetAfterIt.

After a lot of internal work, I have come to believe that living an authentic life has to be about making intentional choices. Being intentional with my time and energy has helped me design a lifestyle that benefited me.

Every day is different. Some days it's focusing on the fresh start. Other days, it's about learning to trust myself; it's doing what I love because it sets my soul on fire; it's cultivating a deeper relationship with myself; it's surrounding myself with people that inspire and elevate me; it's listening to podcasts and audiobooks that strengthen my core value system; it's reading books about other people's journeys. And it's remembering that perfection feeds into anxiety, which breeds fear, and that it does not define me.

But it wasn't always that easy. For years, Anxiety and Perfection were my two closest frenemies.

Anxiety was like a high school dance partner I didn't choose. She plucked me from the sidelines and placed her hands on my body as if to reassure me she was doing me a favor. Then she'd spin me into the arms of Perfection.

In the beginning, they both would lead, but I've since learned the dance myself.

And through all the push and pull in the dance of life, I have let the friction, the resistance, callus and harden me. Whenever I look at my hands now, I'm humbled by my grit, discipline, and strength.

If you've ever seen *The Return to OZ*, I'd reckon my journey was similar to that yellow brick road.

I don't doubt that your journey will differ from mine. More often than not, we won't know where we will end up until we get there. In the past, I used to think that the grass was greener on the other side but I could not be more wrong. I learned that it's greener where we water it—where we tend to and care for it. Because just like a garden, you need to know what you're growing. That is how I mastered my mind.

CUT THE SH*T

On July 1, 2015, I quit smoking.

This decision created the largest domino effect my life had ever seen—in the best way possible.

This vice had nuzzled itself between my fore and middle finger for about five years. Then I decided that enough was enough: I would quit smoking cold-turkey. The night before I quit—midnight was close. I headed to the corner store at the end of my street and picked up a pack of Belmont. I wanted to feel the smoke fill, cradle, and hold my lungs captive one more time.

For the next three months, I carried that same pack of Belmont with me everywhere. It was like I put myself on probation to test my willpower and to see who was stronger: me or the nicotine. The only thing that made it easier during this time was the amount of encouragement I had from my support system. When I showed them strength, they awed. And when I showed them weakness, they bolstered me up.

Then I quit drinking. I quit hanging out with friends who were not impacting my lifestyle in a healthy or positive way. I quit doing things I had no interest in. I quit living up to other people's expectations of me. I quit believing people who told me no. I quit letting negativity dictate and change my mood. And most importantly, I quit doubting myself.

It took my first commitment to myself to spring my whole life back into motion. I said "yes" to quitting smoking and I surprised myself. People used to tell me I had an addictive personality but I didn't do this to prove them wrong. I was proving myself right: I could do whatever I set my mind on. I was astonished by how much more clearly I saw, how much better food tasted, and how the air could hug my depleted lungs until they knew how to blush again. When I looked in the mirror, fourteen-year-old Annie smiled back.

I knew I was on the right track because I felt her pride in my strides forward.

MASTER YOUR MIND

As a tomboy, I was always invested in sports and anything that got me to sweat.

Playing on teams had a much larger influence on how I live my life than I knew at the time. It taught me what teamwork means. It taught me to value and respect my competition. It taught me to believe in myself. It taught me how showing up and being consistent is how we get after it. And it taught me: no pain, no gain.

In gym class, I would run until everyone else had stopped, then run an extra lap before collapsing. I was in my state of "psychological warfare" (a concept I learned from Jocko Willink, a retired Navy SEAL officer and host of Jocko Podcast). It didn't matter if my shins felt like they were being ripped open, if my lungs couldn't hold onto the oxygen for long, if I had sweat pouring into my eyes.

These self-indulgent uncomfortable experiences made me tougher and more resilient than ever.

Yes, I'm a bit of a weirdo: I'm motivated by temporary suffering or pressure. It's like an internal bat signal. If my brain has switched it on, I don't ask questions, I just do whatever it takes.

But we'll talk more about mental discipline in a couple of paragraphs. First let's talk about physical discipline.

I work out four or five times a week.

The gym is my sanctuary. It's a place I go to detox my mind, body, and soul. It also helps me develop discipline and calluses my mind and body to tackle the daily grind. As Jocko Willink puts it: discipline equals freedom.

The commitment to yourself is how you hold yourself accountable.

I love using the gym as an example of how we can become who we want to be. Weight loss, lean muscle, bulking up, isolating muscle groups: these need consistent effort. I used the same mentality to design a life I can be proud of living.

So how do we build a lifestyle? By mastering our minds.

There's no "one way" to master the mind, everyone is different. But for me, I find setting intentions at the start of my day helpful in keeping me aligned with my goals. Whether they are long-term or short-term goals, it's like I have a mood board for my design of life. Setting intentions has also helped me begin with more gratitude, positive thoughts, and compassion—like a mental framework to decide which thoughts can stay and which need to leave in order for me to be productive.

Being aware of how I'm living my life makes it easier to *choose* to lead the best life possible. I encourage anyone—night owl or early riser—to make setting intentions part of your routine. I can tell you that I'm not only more productive, but I also have higher energy levels and my foresight is 20/20.

Mastering your mind is comparable to tending to your own garden.

PRESSURE MAKES DIAMONDS

My parents told me once, there are two kinds of people in the world: worker bees and social butterflies.

I like to align myself with a bee-butterfly hybrid. But whenever I hit a roadblock, my father—with all the love in his heart—would call me a "无头苍蝇" (direct translation: a headless fly). It was a metaphor he used to describe someone who skated through life unencumbered by a lack of direction.

In hindsight, he wasn't wrong.

I tend to be an impulsive person: ideas, actions, decisions, purchases, relationships. I know I don't always make the best choices or use of my time. My decisions all start with a burning desire or passion but that can diminish quickly. It can sometimes feel demotivating to have to hold onto that feeling, and when I'm off that high, that's when my brain goes into *Procrastination Mode*.

In *Procrastination Mode*, I default to doing anything but what I need to do. No lie, I struggled to focus on writing this chapter. I worked on poetry, writing blog posts, reading books, and practicing the guitar. And I wrote so many variations of this chapter.

But I decided I need to look at procrastination differently, so I did.

Turns out, procrastination isn't all bad. I discovered my innate ability to work and perform under pressure with ease. And the adrenaline rush of doing something last-minute is irreplaceable.

It's all about perspective. How you look at things will affect how you respond to them. For me, procrastination is a daily struggle, but I get by with a little help from people who inspire me. Maya Angelou has immortalized this reminder on my fridge: "Nothing will work unless you do."

Now, I was born in the month of April which means that my birthstone is a diamond. It's also my favorite kind of gemstone. Diamonds are crystal clear and are created through immense pressure and heat; if you apply the same to life—failure, obstacles, and suffering are just another way of becoming something new.

In one short year, I did more than I thought I could. *Hello, lead UX designer, Co-Founder of the Women United Project, and a co-author of this book.* The pay-off of not doing anything to change my situation was too high. Ergo, I've been saying "Pressure makes diamonds" for a long time. It's even the subtitle for this part of my chapter. Only this time around, I apply the same concept of how a diamond is made to design a life I was proud of living.

COMMITTED TO CHANGE

When I was younger, I had a lot of issues with commitment—but I was enthralled by it, too. Some said it was fear, others said I just hadn't found "it" yet. Whatever "it" was, I was willing to spend a lifetime searching for.

There's a saying that goes: the more you look for it, the harder it is to find. My mother says it's like asking Buddha for a comb. So, when I decided to stop looking for "it" at twenty-three years old, I found myself in a long-term live-in relationship.

At the time, I thought I'd found "The One" when, in fact, this was only the beginning of my journey. It was like a game of Minesweepers riddled with red flags. And because I loved him, I decided to stay and play the game. I carefully danced around the flags that might undo everything we've worked at—I worked at.

Being in that relationship, I learned a lot about myself but it drained me. I felt pressured to play the part of the perfect girl-friend. From the outside, it looked like I had it altogether. On the inside, I was frantically feeling my way through the darkness. And the more time I spent hiding behind the mask, the less of me there was left.

For me, my greatest blessing—and possibly, curse—is that I have the ability to romanticize every detail of my life. It helped make life more tolerable. *Who doesn't want to walk around smiling and believing fully, and wholly, that everything will work out?* The challenging part was I had a hard time getting myself unstuck because I wasn't able to express myself genuinely.

Over time, it got progressively harder to romanticize the events that unfolded in that Queen West apartment we lived in. And by the time we moved to the East end, we basically became roommates. We ate together once a week. Date nights happened less frequently. We worked opposite hours and hardly slept in the same bed together. He made all the decisions and never asked for my opinion. All the while, I lived in fear of his disappointment of my true self.

As I spiralled deeper, I remember thinking, "This can't be it."

Then, I had a breakthrough: the only person capable of changing my life for the better was me. So, I did.

When I was in an unhealthy relationship, *I left it.*

When my job was uninspiring, *I changed it.*

When I wasn't feeling good about myself, *I hit the gym.*

When busy wasn't productive, *I reprioritized things.*

Whenever anxiety tried to hold me down, *I focused on gratitude.*

The first rule of committing to change is:

FEEL THE FEAR AND DO IT ANYWAY.

For too long fear controlled me when it should've been my compass. It was letting me know that whatever I was about to do, there are consequences but greatness also lies ahead. I focused on where I was going and what I was committed to in my life, and what I was creating.

I know it's easier than it sounds but I took my time to sit with fear. I didn't let it rush how I processed my emotions, feelings, or experiences. Instead, I let it help me prepare to tackle the obstacles I'll face. Whatever story fear was telling me, I knew it was better than to be shrinking to fit places I've outgrown.

There's no shame in starting over or falling as long as you rise again.

I learned that in order for me to reach someplace new, I had to do something different than what I've always done. If I did the same thing everyday, the same results would show up and nothing in my situation will ever, would never change. It's through changing the conversation with myself that I witnessed the power of language moves.

That is how I mastered my mind.

We're all capable of it when we give ourselves permission to change, adapt, grow, get better. Is change scary sometimes? *Yes.* Did I wish things would stay the same sometimes? *Also, yes.* But is sacrificing the "could haves" worth it so I can live and deserve better? *A million times, yes!*

When I committed to change, everything I looked at started to look different. Instead of fighting and resisting change, I surrendered to it. Maybe, I even embraced it. And if I failed, it became a lesson that I learned from. That is growth. From fear ruling my mind to fear being my drive, I became everything I ever wanted to be.

Changing the language I spoke to myself with made all the difference in my life. It changed how I thought about myself, and changed the story I was living. I didn't know what was on the other side of fear, but I knew it was a new beginning. And regardless of what society dictated I'd be at this age, I was willing—ready to begin, again.

The fact is one commitment to myself created a paradigm-shifting domino effect.

It began with recognizing the fact that I was no longer the main character of my own story. And when you're living a life that's no longer yours to control, know that it's okay to leave whatever is holding you back. There had been moments when I wasn't ready to realize my own growth but being patient and kind to yourself is what will help you get to where you need to be.

It's through fear that I learned that change is inevitable. It's growth. It's progression. It's part of life. It's a choice I make waking up every day. It's by mastering our minds can we then embrace our fears, our feelings, and our actions—and realize that the grass is greener where we water it.

Because this is 100% me being resolute and standing in my *own* truth.

CHAPTER 6

CHOICES, CHANCES, CHANGES

*"What would you do if you knew
there was no possibility of failing?"*

THERESA TOSCANO

Theresa is a successful entrepreneur who believes in the law of attraction and that the energy you put out into the universe is what you get back.

She currently resides in Rochester, NY where she was born and raised. For fourteen years, she lived in the Philadelphia area and enjoyed many summers at the Jersey shore. In 2000, Theresa adopted two pups who ran her household for the next fifteen years! She is passionate about animal welfare and fosters dogs and dreams of one day having a sanctuary for senior dogs so they don't have to live their last days out in a shelter.

Theresa's professional background is in human resources; however, in 2014 while scrolling through Facebook, she saw a random post that forever changed her life! After a short conversation (with someone she didn't know!), she took a blind leap of faith on a new entrepreneurial journey that has helped her grow and become a better version of herself. Now Theresa's mission is to help other women do the same.

ig: @theresatoscano.llc | fb: @theresatoscanoLLC
li: @theresatoscanoLLC

What would you do if you knew there was no possibility of failing? Would your life be different?

Everyone dreams about who they want to be or what they want to do in life. Some people pursue their dream, others attempt it and give up, and then there are those who never even try. What holds these people back?

There are lots of excuses we hide behind: I'm too old, too young, don't have the money, too busy, it's not the right time, etc. Or maybe we allow the people in our circle to have more influence over our decisions than they should. While these might seem like justified reasons, ultimately, a lack of action almost always comes down to self-doubt and fear. When we base our decisions on fear or insecurity instead of purpose or love, we give our power away to the negative story we've created in our head.

Fear of failure, fear of rejection, fear of the unknown, or fear of being judged can shatter dreams. I felt all of these when I decided to start a business. There I was with a new bachelor's degree, wondering whether people would think I was crazy for not using my education. Then I heard somebody say that unless someone is paying your bills, you shouldn't be concerned with what they think about how you make a living. I knew that if I tried my best and it didn't work out, I would be ok. But if I didn't try at all, would I always wonder, "What if?"

So many wildly successful people have failed repeatedly before they found success, but they didn't allow fear of failure to keep them from pushing forward with their dream; maybe they even used fear of missing out to push them time and time again. If they had given up, we would not have KFC, Macy's, Ford, Harry Potter, or Disney, just to name a few!

TAKING THE LEAP

"In the end, we only regret the chances we didn't take." ~Lewis Carroll

When I started working in the Human Resources department of a radiology company, I felt like I had found my niche. As a people-person, having a job where I got to interact with all the employees was right up my alley. I enjoyed it and had decided HR would be my career path until I retired. *So I thought.* Unfortunately, within a five-year period, I was laid off from three different companies due to downsizing. I felt disheartened and wasn't sure whether staying in this field was the best decision, but I had many years of experience at that point and still felt like HR was such a great fit for me. Knowing that a bachelor's degree would make me more marketable to employers, I enrolled in college. I had every intention of going back into the human resources field when I graduated, but apparently God had other plans for me. On the evening of my very last day of school, a completely different opportunity fell in my lap.

I stumbled across a new company that was still in pre-launch so there wasn't a lot of information available. The only details shared with me was that they offered luxury hair care products through the direct sales business model, and if I enrolled before the official launch the next day (no pressure!), I was eligible to become a Founder and earn quarterly revenue-share bonuses.

My first thought was, "Well, I've been in direct sales once before and didn't have any success, so why would this be different?" Plus I had just spent two years finishing my bachelor's degree and was eager to get back to work. Clearly, the logical choice would have been to dismiss the opportunity and say no thank you.

But something about the opportunity to be a Founder intrigued me, and the fact that no other company in the direct sales industry focused on hair care meant that this could be different.

So I decided, "What have I got to lose?" The worst-case scenario would be that I'd get a box of healthy hair care at a great discount, but I never dreamed that the best-case scenario could be that this company would change my life. At 11:45pm, with fifteen minutes to spare, I jumped in!

As excited as I was, I immediately felt self-doubt creeping in. The truth is, I'm not a "salesperson." But as I learned more about the company, the products, and the perks of financial and time freedom, that doubt started to turn into motivation. I decided to commit to learning how to be successful in this business so I would never have to go back to a corporate job and worry about being laid off again. For the next full year, I put my head down and went to work. All my effort paid off and exactly one year later, I became a Founder!

The lesson I took away from this experience is to not let a fear of the unknown get in my way. It is possible to make a spontaneous decision with very little information that could end up being one of the best decisions of your life!

THE MENTALITY SHIFT

When I stepped away from the corporate world to become a full-time entrepreneur, I didn't think about the changes I'd need to make, both in my daily habits and in the way I thought.

Since I had always worked for an employer, I was "employee-minded," which differs greatly from being "business-minded." The transition did not happen overnight. It took me a while to adjust to being my own boss. Truth be told, I'm still figuring some things out! These are a few of the challenges . . .

Work-Life Balance. No longer having to "punch a time clock" brings with it an incredible sense of freedom. But how you manage your time when you work from home can impact your business in a big way. There are so many built-in distractions at home, and it takes a lot of self-discipline to stay focused on income-producing activities. This was, and still is, one of the hardest things for me to control.

A few things that have helped include having a routine, creating a realistic to-do list, time-blocking my day (check out the Pomodoro Technique), setting boundaries to reduce interruptions, and having a specific work area/office. And I no longer have a television in my house. Yes, seriously.

Just me, myself, and I. Working from home can get lonely. I was used to seeing people all the time and missed that connection. To help combat the isolation, I have joined a couple of networking groups that meet once a month. I also got a part-time job that gets me out of the house a couple nights a week.

Accountability. As an employee, we typically have a set of specific responsibilities that fall within the scope of our job and a superior who reviews our performance on a regular basis. We get feedback on where we need to develop and suggestions on how to improve, and we always have someone to give us direction when needed. As a business owner, though, you are solely responsible for all decisions—big or small, good or bad. Business owners also have to identify their own strengths and weaknesses and create a plan for growth and success.

Progress vs. perfection. As a human resource professional, I was somewhat of a perfectionist with my work; I was very thorough and tried my best to avoid mistakes. As an entrepreneur, that isn't possible. You try something, see how it works, modify if needed, and try again. I had to change the way I felt about being wrong and embrace the concept that mistakes are okay; I needed to focus on growth over results. As an employee, I thought of failure as the opposite of success. As an entrepreneur, I've learned that it's actually an important part of success.

The expert in anything was once a beginner who learned through practice and failure.

> *"Failure is only the opportunity to begin again more intelligently."* ~Henry Ford

LEARNING TO LEAD

> *"If your actions inspire others to dream more, learn more, do more, and become more, you are a leader."* ~John Quincy Adams

About a month into my entrepreneurial journey, I enrolled my first team member. On that day I became a leader! I'd had no real leadership training, but since I wanted to build a team, I had to learn how to lead them. I immediately started following some of the top mentors in the industry, people like Jim Rohn, Darren Hardy, and Eric Worre. I asked other leaders for book recommendations and found a lot of great training on YouTube. I also tuned in to other successful leaders in our company to learn what they were doing. If it was working for them, why reinvent the wheel?

I was like a sponge, absorbing all this new information so I could pass it on and provide value to my team. For me to have success, I had to help others build their success first. This is actually one of my favorite things about this industry! I wanted my team members to know that we are in this together and that they'll always have someone cheering them on to reach their goals.

As my team grew and I started experiencing success, the light bulb went on and it hit me—*I have a gift that can change people's lives!* Even if that meant only making an extra $500 a month, I could show them how to do it! I became passionate about inspiring my team to have a clear vision of what could be and to set goals for what they wanted out of their business. Hence, we are called Team Inspire!

Like everything else in life, you have to have the right mindset to achieve success in business. Entrepreneurship, particularly in direct sales, is a rollercoaster ride full of ups and downs and honestly, a lot of rejection. Without the ability to discipline the disappointments, most people will quit. So on my team, self-development is a non-negotiable task. Not only does this development provide us with tools and skills to push through the downs, it has a positive impact on every other aspect of our lives.

Success isn't just about how much money you make or how big your business is: it's about who you become along the journey. The person I am today is definitely not who I would be if I hadn't started this business. And it's not just me. I have seen so much personal growth in others that sometimes I feel like we are a self-development company that just happens to sell hair and skin care products!

Jim Rohn said, "Income seldom exceeds personal development. If you took all the money in the world and divided it equally among everybody, it would soon be back in the same pockets it was before. Therein lies the simple key to growing your income—growing yourself!"

NEVER SAY NEVER

Becoming an entrepreneur was not something I was actively seeking or even thinking about doing, but I am beyond grateful that the opportunity was put in my path. Would I have been happy if I had continued my career in the corporate world? Perhaps. But thinking about all the incredible things I've experienced and the amazing people I've met, I could not imagine any other life than this one.

As my team continues to grow, it is so fulfilling to see how many lives I'm impacting because I tried something out of my comfort zone. Sometimes I wonder, "What if I had said no?" Not only would my life be much different, so would the lives of hundreds of other women.

When someone doesn't have enough faith in themselves to believe they can succeed, they settle. Do you wake up dreading the day? Have you ever had a gut feeling that you were meant for something more, or wondered "What if?" Don't let self-doubt or fear keep you from exploring a new path in life. Nothing is ever set in stone.

Assess where you are and where you'd like to be. What do you love? What are you passionate about? What excites you? What are you good at? You can make any of these things into a career. Listen to your intuition and then action. What is one small step you can take today that will get you closer to a more joyful and grateful life? Hold yourself accountable and do it.

WHAT NOT TO DO

Don't put it off until you're ready. There will never be a "perfect time"—it simply doesn't exist! If something is important to you, make it a priority. Don't let money be a roadblock; if you want something badly enough, get creative about how to come up with the funds to do it. Don't compare yourself to others, and stop worrying about what other people will think! Not everyone will support you, so just surround yourself with those who do.

And lastly, in the words of Earl Nightingale: *"Never give up on a dream just because of the time it will take to accomplish it. The time will pass anyway."*

When we make a choice and take a chance, we could be one decision away from changing our life!

CHAPTER 7

A WOMAN'S PLACE IS EVERYWHERE

"Get comfortable with beinguncomfortable! Success can only be achieved by being willing to step outside of your comfort zone."

LORI ARMITAGE

Lori Armitage is a motivated, dynamic leader with over ten years of successful sales management for Essity, a global professional hygiene company. She is a devoted wife to her husband Dan and mother to two golden retrievers, Utah and Quincey. Lori is a high-energy, hands-on sales manager with the ability to teach, mentor, and motivate her team, resulting in high performance results year over year. She is a seven-time Sales Award Winner and was recognized as one of the Top 50 Most Inspiring Employees globally in her organization. Her passions include travelling, attending rock concerts, playing hockey, and golfing. She loves spending time with family and friends and is known as the "Hostess of the Mostess." She is a social coordinator and an unofficial party planner—a good time is sure to follow wherever Lori goes. To quote her kindergarten teacher, "Lori has an incredible 'Joie de Vivre' (Joy of Living)" which has followed her throughout her life. Lori loves change and embraces new challenges, both good and bad. She believes everything happens for a reason and that negative experiences and loss can only make you stronger, more resilient, and more appreciative of life and love.

ig: armitagelori4 | fb: Lori Hicks-Armitage
li: Lori Hicks-Armitage | t: @armitagelori4

When I look back on my childhood, it is absolutely no sur-prise that my life turned out the way that it has. When I played make-believe, I always told the story of living on my own with my dog, playing office or school and coming home at night to *my* condo. I was far too busy make-believe working that it wasn't even imaginable that I was ever going to be a homemaker or a mother.

I was the youngest of two with a brother 4.5 years older than me; my mother worked evenings as a nurse, leaving my dad as our af-ter-school caregiver, meal prepper, tutor, chauffeur and coach three to four nights a week. This was a busy time indeed for my family, with my parents constantly doing the balancing act of making sure we attended all of our extra-curricular activities while still ensuring we were doing our homework and practicing our musical instruments. Parenting then was all about raising successful young adults, prepar-ing us for adulthood, disappointment, and of course, success.

Despite our age difference, I considered my brother my very best friend (and still do today). I was the typical annoying little sis-ter, following him everywhere, wanting and pretending to be older to fit in with him and his friends. Our neighbourhood was domi-nated by boys and a few girls who were closer to my brother's age than my own, so my childhood could also be very lonely at times. It was a different time back then: parents did not arrange playdates at any age, and they certainly didn't appreciate playdates that re-quired them to have to drive us and pick us up. You walked or rode your bike, or it didn't happen. This of course wasn't a bad thing, as it drove me to become wildly independent, creating my own games of house, school, and office using my stuffed animals (*not* dolls) as my students, co-workers, and friends.

When I was around seven, my mother started to get very involved with the nurse's union at the Ottawa Civic Hospital. There was a nurses' strike around that time and my brother came home singing "We're Not Gonna Take It" by Twisted Sister. The very first time my mother heard that song, she said, "I am bringing that to the picket line tomorrow!" She had us making signs and walking the picket line alongside her and the other nurses, with my brother's Ghetto Blaster boombox blaring Twisted Sister as loud as it could go! I was too young to be embarrassed and too naive to be proud. The most exciting moment of that entire time was when my mom got interviewed by CTV and said right into the cameras, "We're just not going to take it anymore." I smile now even as I write this . . . she was amazing.

My mother's passion for the union and what it stood for grew within her, eventually leading her to apply for a full-time position at the Ontario Nurses Association Head Office in Toronto. My mother worked for ONA for over twenty years—giving it her everything. She was determined to make a difference both for the nurses she represented and for the organization as a whole.

Mom ingrained in us to never stop learning or trying to better ourselves. One of my mother's proudest and greatest achievements (in addition to earning her university degree in her fifties) was being selected as one of 218 Delegates (out of four thousand applicants) for the Governor General's Study Conference in 1987. She was selected because she demonstrated "leadership qualities and signs of upward mobility." She travelled across Canada for eighteen days trying to figure out why the country was so difficult to govern, what could be done to make it better and what other Canadians really cared about. As a young female tween, it was such an honor for me to have this positive role model as a parent. She taught both my brother and me that you have to fight for what you want in life; you need to work hard; you have to be willing to take risks; and that "shockingly," life can be difficult at times.

Being a working woman in the '80s—a time of great change for women—my mother also instilled in me that men and women deserve the same rights and opportunities,especially in the workplace. She taught me to never settle for anything less and to always fight for what I believe in.

Sadly my mother recently lost her final fight. Eight years ago, my beautiful, vivacious, and tenacious mother was diagnosed with a very rare brain disease called Progressive Supranuclear Palsy—a form of ALS, dementia, and Parkinson's combined. She fought a great fight with dignity and grace to the very end.

I will always be eternally grateful for how my mother raised me. It was she who taught me how to succeed and persevere in this "Man's World," to never give up and to believe that I *am* equal. Together, she and my father showed both my brother and me that there are no gender roles in relationships, parenting, or the workplace. They both prepared me for the harsh reality of the world being a male-dominated environment and to expect to work harder to be that "Boss Lady" I so desired to be.

These lessons have served me well-especially being a woman leader in a male-dominated industry; it has taught me so much about myself, about men, about women, and about how to successfully survive in a cut-throat, dog-eat-dog world. The women I have encountered and worked with over the years that have been successful within this industry all have the same qualities in common: we know how to play the game and *win*. We know when to take a joke and when to throw it back. We command respect and deliver the results that earn it. We know we need to plan ahead and be strategic with our approach and proposals of execution. Women who succeed are aware that they will be judged differently and that we may need to work harder to earn the same respect as a man in a similar position. As Sheryl Sandberg discusses in *Lean In*, women first have to be "likeable" in order to be viewed as successful. I recently experienced a situation where a female Senior Vice President was coming up from the U.S. to their Canadian manufacturing facility with the mandated role of "getting the plant back on track." Rather than the employees being excited for her and the potential changes she would be bringing, the comments surrounding her visit were extremely derogatory, sexist, and disappointing. Because this person was a female, it was automatically assumed by both male and female employees across all levels of senior-ity that she would be "unlikeable, bossy, and difficult" and that "SHE better not think she can come in here and just start changing things"—despite the fact that this was precisely what she had been hired to do. If it had been a man coming in "to change things," it might have been viewed as more needed/warranted.

Being able to overcome these gender biases, to let them roll off your back, to prove them wrong, and to be likeable *and* suc-cessful is what sets female leaders apart from their male counter-parts. Having to work harder for that respect and recognition goes hand-in-hand with a feeling of great self-worth, self-discovery, and personal strength.

> *"We know that gender equality isn't just a social issue; it's a business imperative. There is plenty of research showing the business case for equality, such as gender-diverse teams are more profitable and innovative; organizations that embrace fe-male-specific issues have higher employee satis-faction and less staff turnover and companies that elevate women are more effective in all dimen-sions."* ~Shelley Zallis

So now the big question becomes—why do companies benefit from promoting women throughout an organization? I believe it is our "feminine" qualities that make women exceptional leaders. Women are naturally more compassionate, empathetic, and nur-turing, all of which allows us to relate well to the people we are managing. We are nimble and excel at multitasking in all aspects of our lives. We are strategic and efficient with how we spend our time. We are fixers who want to help an employee overcome what-ever hurdles they are experiencing and want to see them excel at the end of it all. We are maternal and see our employees' positive performance as a direct reflection of our leadership.

I felt all of this first-hand when I moved into a leadership role. I started at my company as a territory manager, successfully achieving my sales goals year after year. Seven years in, the "sales manager" role became available and I threw my hat in the ring. I was *extremely* nervous and stumbled over many of my responses during the interview process, but my hiring managers were thankfully able to see past the nerves and were able to catch a glimpse of my leadership potential.

Moving from being my team's peer to being their manager was a very daunting task, and one that I did not take lightly. I was stepping away from my comfort zone and entering into a world of unknown, where my future success was no longer solely dependent on me and my own actions but instead dependent on how I coached and trained and guided others. I quickly adapted my individual approach with each of my team members, attempting to remain their friend while still providing advice and guidance in a tactful and purposeful way. I still use words like "we" and "us"; I have never viewed myself as superior to my team—instead I consider myself an extension of the team who is here to help us be successful together.

All that being said, it wasn't always easy, and my first few years as a manager were very challenging. I had taken over the role of a man who was positively adored and thoroughly admired and respected by the team and our customers. Despite the fact that he was still with the company and still completely accessible whenever needed, there was an initial bout of bitterness, a non-acceptance, and a certain level of questionable doubt in my competency as a leader. Early on I, too, was experiencing feelings of self-doubt, anger, bitterness, and jealousy; I felt unappreciated, undervalued, and at times outright resentful. I had gone from being a top salesperson to a questionable sales manager, and despite winning an award my first year in the management role, I still didn't feel it was "*my*" district, I didn't feel that they were "*my*" customers, and I certainly didn't feel that any of this success was due to any of "*my*" efforts. I was going through all of this unbeknownst to my boss (the man I had replaced) and also unbeknownst to my team. It was a daily battle within my own mind, and I had no one to confide in or vent to.

Never had I dreamed that replacing someone would have been such a difficult challenge, but like with everything in life, the transition just took time. As I gained experience through both positive and negative situations, it got easier. As I hired new people whom I got to train and mold in my own way, it got easier. As I continued under the guidance and leadership of my boss, both my customers and my team began to realize that this change wasn't so bad, and I began to gain the recognition (and the reputation) that "this girl gets things done." Eventually I became the go-to person for my customers and my direct reports. I accepted that my boss and all his "likeability" was not a threat to me in my new role; instead, he was my greatest ally, supporter, and friend. His trust and belief in me has been like none other I have ever experienced in my life and without it, I truly would not be where I am today.

Through years of delivering on results and helping my company, my sales representatives, and my customers' businesses grow, so did my confidence and pride in the job that I do. One of our Vice Presidents recently told me that my greatest weakness has always been doubt in myself and my own capabilities—I myself am not aware of the positive influence I have on others and the job that I do. It has taken a very long time for me to realize that I truly can accomplish whatever it is I set my mind to—including being a published writer!

Despite it being a rocky road at times, my ability to overcome these challenges and learning to believe in myself; to apply my own personal approach and my own ways of doing things is truly what has defined my success. I never allowed the fact that I was in a male-dominated industry to negatively influence me or cause me to falter in any way; instead I chose to embrace the positive influence of my amazing male role models and mentors and allow them to help guide me through my career. I chose to make a name for myself in this industry and to prove to myself and the naysayers that women can survive and thrive in this industry—and have a lot of fun doing it!

So if I can provide any advice to other women it would be the following: Believe in yourself, find your own voice and your own approach; be willing to take risks and to stand up for what you believe in. Always be accountable for your actions—stand behind them and *own* them. Remember when you make a mistake, there are three things you should always do: admit it, learn from it, and don't repeat it. Find your mentors and role models—male or female—and embrace their knowledge and advice; always be open to learning new things. Be confident (but not too confident), be likable, stay humble, and always be respectful of others—*especially other women.* Like the Facebook meme says: "Be the woman who adjusts another woman's crown without ever mentioning it was crooked."

As women, we must support and encourage other women : we need to congratulate and *elevate* one another. We need to silence our own jealousy and insecurities and be proud of our female peers and other women in leadership roles. Women can truly be our own worst enemies; we need to change this narrative and become each other's biggest allies. After all, if we don't believe in, respect, and support other women—why should we ever expect men to?

HEART

RISE WITH LOVE

CHAPTER 8

TRANSFORMATIVE MINDSET: TURNING TRAUMA INTO POWER

"There is only one you and you have something special to give and contribute to the world, no matter how big or small. You just have to dig deep, believe, and find yourself—because the best is yet to come!"

STEPH CLARK

Steph Clark is a make-up artist, glow specialist, and jill-of-all trades. She has done everything from assistant hat design and concert promotion to dog walking and kitchen management. Her passion is helping women feel beautiful on the inside and out. She uses her empathic nature to empower women to realize their full potential.

As a big thinker and dreamer, Steph believes anything is possible. From an early age, she was a problem solver and enjoyed helping others achieve their goals. So naturally, she received her goal coaching certificate so she could use her knowledge to help others develop a positive mindset and make the changes they needed to succeed.

Steph loves people and her community and is a natural people connector. It is her hope to help women around the world live out the life they want and and were meant to have. She is working toward building a global brand that brings women together so that they can build confidence, love, and encouragement as a whole.

Steph resides in Ontario with her two children and her husband. She looks forward to being a role model for her children and providing them with amazing experiences and life lessons.

www.stephkmua.com
ig:@stephkmua | fb:@stephkmua | li: steph-k-919a43185

As a little girl, I had a huge imagination. I thrived whenever I was creating. As I developed, I found my spark, my passion—I wanted to be a singer. I would imagine what it would be like to sing in front of thousands as I belted out my fav Mariah songs. In high school, when *American Idol* launched, I would sit on the edge of my seat with tears in my eyes as I watched the performers. I knew their deep desire, and I shared their passion, that undeniable feeling of wanting a dream to come true more than anything! It was like the stars aligned when the show came to Canada. When the day came for me to audition, I was so nervous. I waited in line for hours, but when my chance came to sing, just like that I was told, "Sorry, you're not what we are looking for." I left the room with tears streaming down my face. It felt like the end of the world.

I was sixteen and my dreams of being the next star were shattered. Maybe it was hormones, my lack of life experience, I'm not sure. But for years, I let that one moment defeat me. My spirit had been broken into a million pieces. From that point on, I began to be more of a realist and let others' opinions reflect my own thoughts and beliefs.

Isn't it crazy how one single moment in time can change not only our whole course of action but also who we are? How it can take away the raw passion that makes our eyes sparkle with excitement when we talk about the thing that we love? As women especially, it is so easy to lose ourselves because of guilt, trauma, our life experiences, and of course—what others will think.

I was lucky enough to have supportive parents and a positive attitude to support me, but it still took traumatic experiences, years of working on myself, and lots of digging deep to discover who I really was beneath the layers of grief.

As a creative mind, I have been gifted with an incredible amount of passion for many different things; I consider myself a free spirit in this regard. My journey of self-discovery truly began after college. I was stoked to be on the right path to finally achieve my dream of becoming a recording artist. With an entertainment management diploma in hand, I desperately tried to find employment in my industry to pay down my daunting student loans. Months passed and I began to lose hope. The thought, "What am I doing with my life?" was the daily track on repeat in my head. At nineteen, I wasn't even close to midlife but I was convinced I was having a crisis. I felt depressed, like my whole purpose had deflated. Finally, I landed a job at a local health food store, where I was quickly promoted to kitchen manager. This would mark the start of the next traumatic experience.

One night while I was driving home, my hands started sweating and I suddenly became extremely anxious. I kept thinking, "It's okay, just get home." I got home and shut myself in my room, but I felt like I was going to die in my sleep. I didn't tell anyone what had happened—until it happened again and again.

For the next year and a half, I experienced severe panic attacks and anxiety. I dropped twenty pounds, barely ate, stayed up until 3am every night, and felt like I was slowly dying. I was so weak and had zero motivation. It felt like I was in a shell watching myself from above. After getting to my wits end, I decided I couldn't live like this any longer. Using my knowledge from my experience at the health food store. I was able to get rid of my anxiety and panic attacks through eliminating wheat and adding a B-vitamin supplement to my health regime.

February 28, 2016: a date that will forever be ingrained in my mind and my heart. I was with my husband and daughter at my best friend's house when my cell phone rang; I didn't recognize the number so I let it go to voicemail. When we were headed home, I listened to the message. It was my aunt telling me, "It's your dad, you need to call me right away!" My first thought was, "Oh no! Dad had a heart attack." When I called her back, she said, "It's your dad. He hung himself. I'm so sorry."

You know the scenes in the movies when there's a climactic moment and everything is in slow motion and there's no sound? That's what I experienced first. It wasn't until I realized that I was screaming that it hit me. I couldn't catch my breath. I started panicking. As I tried to process what was happening, my mind went into overdrive. It was by far the most traumatic experience of my life.

I clearly remember the drive to my parents' house that night. It felt like I was on autopilot as we pulled in to see police cars and an ambulance parked by my dad's shop. He was inside. I wanted to run past everyone and make sure it wasn't all just a mistake. Every part of me felt paralyzed, and I didn't know what to do with myself; I stood helplessly in the dark while my mom and brother spoke with the police. When I finally made it home, I felt sick to my stomach and my head was pounding so much that I couldn't see straight. I ran myself a hot bath, submerged my head under the water, and broke down.

The next morning felt like a bad hangover. *Was that just a bad dream?* It took every ounce of strength I had to put on a brave face and continue on. I was in a lot of pain mentally and physically. That September, I became pregnant with my second child; I knew at that moment that I needed to begin my healing process. I booked an appointment with a psychotherapist and began my journey.

I told my therapist that I felt like an imposter, I wasn't happy inside, I was angry and emotional, and my heart was broken, yet I had to continue on with life almost as if nothing had happened for fear that I would push away friends and family. The more I worked on the layers of pain/trauma from not only my dad's passing but from other experiences in my past, the more I began to realize that I could not continue to be a victim of a tragedy. I wasn't just the daughter of a father who took his life. I was a woman who had had big dreams before her life was flipped upside down. At this moment, the shift happened. I had two options: continue to let my grief overcome me, which I was sure would lead to depression, or get back up and continue to heal. I knew my dad would have wanted the latter.

In August 2017 came the next big turning point. I attended a business conference with my family in Florida. It was the first time since my father's death that I felt truly relaxed, I could just be. We floated down a lazy river, ate incredible food, and enjoyed each other's company. My dad was from Jamaica and while I was floating down the lazy river, Bob Marley's "Three Little Birds" came on. I knew it was a sign that "everything was going to be alright."

That weekend, Brandon Barber spoke all about mindset and limiting beliefs. I felt like he was speaking directly to me. The light bulb went on in my head and just like that, everything clicked! This was the start of me realizing what needed to happen for me to achieve my goals and change my life forever.

Not long after the conference, a thought popped into my head: "This had to happen this way." Dad had to do what he did in order for me to become who I was meant to be. I felt terrible as soon as the thought appeared, but as I continued to mull it over, I realized that ever since that horrible night, my perspective on life, people, and my fear of the unknown had changed. I was no longer afraid to be who I was meant to be and was starting to believe that I truly could do all that my heart desired. Sometimes it takes a loss to be found.

I went home with a new bounce in my step, feeling rejuvenated and ready to get back in the saddle and start my business. Being a goal-getter made it easier to figure out where I wanted to begin, but I was hit with overwhelm when I thought of the daunting task of navigating the workload on top of still being in the healing process. Was I truly ready for the ups and downs of entrepreneurship? The phrase "entrepreneurial roller coaster" describes the feeling exactly. I knew that being held accountable, having people with whom I could connect and to whom I could relate would definitely make the mental aspect of entrepreneurship easier. So I set out on a quest to find just that!

THE POWER OF COMMUNITY

Even though I was a quiet child, I've always been a social butterfly. I've always needed the perfect balance of being alone and experiencing life with friends. My first taste of self-employment came after I left my job as an assistant hat designer. I was a contractor for a dog walking company, and I loved every minute of having my own schedule and the freedom it gave me to work on the concert promotion company my husband and I had started. After having my daughter, I decided that my passion for make-up, which had been a hobby since my early teens, was going to be my next venture. One day, I was working online and stumbled across a women's networking group called FemCity. I didn't know much about it; all I knew was that twenty-five women met once a month and worked on growing not only personally but also as business owners. I joined, and the rest is history!

After each FemCity meeting, I felt inspired and ready to take on the world. Not only had I found a group of women who got the daily ups and downs of being an entrepreneur, but I had also found a group of genuine, inspiring women with whom I now have a deep connection as friends! I gained a sense of community and belonging, which has helped me stay focused and find clarity. Best of all, I am continuing to manifest my dreams faster than ever before. I found a space where I was able to share my story, triumphs, and struggles, which helped me so much! FemCity has also increased my network and allowed me to collaborate with amazing businesses in my community.

TIPS TO BUILD YOUR COMMUNITY

1. **Network.** Find a group of like-minded people to meet with (networking groups and book clubs can be good places to start). You can even start your own and meet up at a local coffee shop.

2. **Get support.** Find an accountability partner, someone with whom you can discuss your goals, wins, and challenges and who will be there to encourage and hold you accountable.

HEALING FROM TRAUMA

There is no one-size-fits-all when it comes to healing from trauma; however, I strongly believe that there are some core tools that anyone can use to find what their own healing process looks like.

TOOLS TO BEGIN THE HEALING PROCESS

1. **Talk to someone.** Find a professional whom you feel comfortable speaking with. Therapy was my biggest breakthrough by far, as it allowed me to hear my thoughts out loud and have someone point out my perceptions, as well as enabled me to work through my past. Even if you have not experienced trauma, I still highly recommend therapy—it's a great way to discover things you didn't realize about yourself.

2. **Healthy body, healthy mind.** Take care of yourself because you are worth it! The first thing that we tend to neglect when we are stressed, hurting, busy, etc. is ourselves. This is the worst thing we can do when we are at a low point. Healthy eating and exercise are a vital part of our mental health! So move your body, even if it's just a daily walk, and eat whole and nutritious meals to fuel yourself. If you were to stop taking your car in for daily maintenance, you would find yourself without a working vehicle. Your body is the same.

3. **Release.** In one of my favorite exercises from my therapist, I had to write a letter to my dad saying all the things that I needed to tell him, with no filter, no judgement. Try it! Write a letter to yourself or someone from a traumatic experience. You then seal the letter and in one week open and read it as if you were the other person. Then write the words you want to hear back from them. Seal that letter and again, in one week open it and write your final letter of

response. It took me months to be able to do this, but when I finally did, it was like a weight had been lifted off my shoulders.

POSITIVE MINDSET

One thing that I am so truly grateful for is the ability to change my thoughts and perspective through practicing a positive mindset. This ability has ultimately been the greatest tipping point in my growth. I didn't develop this ability overnight, and it's still a work in progress, but even on my down days, once I am able to throw the tantrum and have the pity party, I am still able to start again and remember all that I am grateful for.

But how do you change your mindset when everything seems to be working against you? You're swimming in bills, your business has hit a plateau, you are just trying to win in the game called life. Have you ever noticed that when you're in a rush in the morning and you start to get flustered, everything seems to go wrong? You spill your coffee trying to get out the door, there's a traffic jam on your way to a meeting, you drop your purse and spill the contents on your way out of the car. We've all been there!

Our mindset and the way we interpret what happens to us play a big part in what we attract! The next time things aren't going as planned, take a deep breath, count to ten, and try and refocus your energy in a positive manner. You'll be surprised at the change in your mood and in your ability to let go and move on with your day!

TIPS FOR PRACTICING A POSITIVE MINDSET

1. **Be inspired.** Set aside a time in your day to say positive affirmations out loud or to listen to or read inspiring podcasts or books. Then take some time and list three things that you are grateful for that day. Try this for at least a week and make a note of the difference in how you feel, your productivity, and your confidence.

2. **Hit the reset button.** I'm not exactly sure where my mom adopted this from, but when I was going through a difficult time and wasn't able to find the positive, my mom would take her finger, press my arm, and say, "Reset." She would then make me change what I had just said into a positive statement. Example: If you find yourself saying things like, "I never have money" or "I can't afford that," take a moment, reset, and rephrase. You could say something like, "I am a money magnet" or "I am open to receive wealth." The more we reinforce the positive, the more we will start to catch ourselves in a limited belief—and flip the script.

* * *

The next process in my journey was goal-setting. This allowed me to see the light at the end of the tunnel, to see that I could be successful while grieving and healing. With each goal accomplished, it was like a small stroke of victory for my broken self, like a piece of the puzzle was being put back together to make me whole again. I was able to feel fulfillment again, excitement for the future, and a sense of pride for inspiring others and being a role model to my children.

GOAL ACTIONS

If I really look back and think about when things changed for me, I can pinpoint the exact moments. One was when I decided to join a book club for Jack Canfield's *The Success Principles*. If you are not familiar with this book, do yourself a favor and read it—it's a total gamechanger! Each has exercises and prompts to help you form strong success habits. The exercise that truly changed my life was the Goal Book, or what I call my Dream Book.

The object of the exercise is to use a binder or journal and dedicate a page to each goal. You use magazine cutouts, words, and pictures that show how your goal will look once it is achieved. Talk about the best way to track your goals! Since starting my dream book over three years ago, I have accomplished my goals faster than ever before!

* * *

One of the hardest things for me weeks after the funeral, when all the family and friends had stopped checking in to see how I was, as they naturally do, was that life goes on. All of the ebb and flow just continues ,and this made me realize that if I didn't keep up with that flow, I would be washed away and left in a darkness that would leave me feeling unfulfilled, unable to inspire and dream. Instead, I chose to use all of the tools I've talked about here to transform my mindset and turn my trauma into power.

As I write these words, it is my hope that you will realize we all have a story. It may be filled with the good, the bad, and the ugly, but it's what makes us uniquely who we are. No matter the cards you are dealt, you deserve to be happy, to be your authentic self, and to live your life to the fullest. There is only one you, and you have something special to give and contribute to the world, no matter how big or small. You just have to dig deep, believe, and find yourself—because the best is yet to come!

CHAPTER 9

TRUSTING YOUR INTUITION

*"When we decide to trust our
instincts and rely on our intuition
to guide us, we open up pathways
to leave second-guessing behind
and embrace the innate power that
resides within us."*

LISA PINNOCK

Lisa is a teacher, musician, mom of two amazing teens (and one funny fur-babe!), and healthy food advocate with Epicure. When she isn't teaching music, leading a choir, or chauffeuring her kids to dance classes, you'll find her doing fun, interactive cooking demos in her community of Markham, Ontario and beyond.

Lisa delved into a leadership role in March 2018 when she founded the FemCity Markham Collective. This group of heart-centred entrepreneurial women connect on a monthly basis to collaborate, support, and lift each other higher, while remaining rooted in the FemCity mantras of gratitude and positivity.

Lisa feels truly honored to be partnering with so many inspirational women on this authoring journey. She believes that self-expression through writing has always been a calling, allowing for a powerful healing process where strength can be uncovered in the midst of vulnerability. She hopes that her experiences and insights will lead other women to a deeper level of self-awareness and empowerment.

ig: @eatwell_withlisa | fb: @eatwell.withlisa
li: @lisa-pinnock-1864a729

When I reflect on my personal evolution, from the time I was a young woman to the present day, a few dominant themes surface over and over. In this life, we get to own what we know to be true. We need to struggle at times and face adversity head-on in order to build resilience, but we don't have to face these moments alone: we can turn to others for support and guidance. And we have an enormous capacity within ourselves to know instinctively which direction to turn in times of need.

I'm honored to share some experiences when I've trusted my intuition, with the hope that you'll be inspired to identify truths about your own unique journey. We all have stories and lessons to share, and we should never underestimate the power they have to positively impact our families, communities, and a world that so desperately needs our light.

In preparation for this book project, some "big questions" kept popping up in my head. For example, where do our intuitive feelings come from? What's the science behind them and how can that knowledge help us? What are the societal norms surrounding the topic of intuition, specifically for women? How can we as women learn to open up to our instincts and access that power? Are there times when we should not rely on our intuition to guide our decisions? If so, how can we know the difference?

Whew, that's a lot of ground to cover in one chapter! So in the spirit of keeping it simple, I chose three inquiry questions as my guideposts: How do we develop our intuitive side? How do we open up to our instinctive nature? And how do we share what we discover by listening to our intuition?

One of my earliest and fondest memories is a bedtime ritual my mom and I developed. We've always shared a special bond and have a remarkably open and honest relationship (well, minus the teenage years, but I'll bet many of us would like to forget those!). At bedtime, she would always come to say prayers with me, and our nighttime prayer routine was a concrete, shining example of faith in action. In retrospect, I realize that her example of living a life grounded in faith made a lasting impression on me. My mom would often encourage me to be still and listen to the voice of God/Jesus/Holy Spirit dwelling within me. I may not have known it at the time, but it was my earliest experience with this type of meditative practice that would provide strength, comfort, and spiritual grounding in my life for years to come. It was also a powerful process that allowed me to begin developing an awareness of my "inner voice" or intuition.

"There are no shortcuts to any place worth going."
~Beverly Sills

Anything worth having takes time and effort to achieve, and that's also the case when learning to access our intuitive skills. For me, it certainly didn't just happen overnight: it took years of being open to those gut feelings and where they might take me. One example from my youth took place during a trip to the movies with people I considered friends at the time. I was about twelve years old and had been part of a Toronto-based opera ensemble for a few years. Socially speaking, I was pretty shy and reserved (except on stage, where I felt most comfortable), and I had high hopes of forging new relationships with the other members of the ensemble. But what became clear that day during our walkabout at the mall was that they didn't want me hanging around at all and were actively trying to lose me before heading into the movie. Decision time: do I continue to look for them and hang on to whatever scraps of company they'd offer, or do I leave on my own and head back home with my dignity intact? Of course, this internal conversation didn't sound so calm and logical in my twelve-year-old brain! But I chose Door Number Two, and to this day, I still remember the look on my mom's face when I told her what had taken place. She told me how proud she was of my actions and how brave I had been to leave the situation. Later that night, she asked what led me to make that decision, with no one else there to guide me. According to my mom's recounting, I replied, "It just didn't feel right . . . I don't think they're all mean kids, but what they were doing was mean, and I didn't want to be treated that way. So I left."

Thinking back to this incident generated further questions for my adult self: How can we as women learn to open up to our intuitive selves? Working from the notion that our intuition has always been there from birth, how do we access it when needed? This is where one of my favorite words comes into play: vulnerability. It's a word that can have such varying meanings and can garner such strong reactions, both positive and negative. My thoughts on being vulnerable are two-fold. I believe it starts with surrendering— perhaps it could be to a higher power or to a belief or conviction you hold near and dear to your heart by accepting that we can't do it all on our own.

The second important step is learning to trust yourself, and that's much easier said than done for many of us. From a young age, we're often taught not to trust our instincts but rather to rely on logic as our guide. I don't believe that we, as women, are wired that way, and denying this innate truth within us can lead to anxiety and tension in our headspace.

> "Vulnerability is not weakness; it's our greatest measure of courage." ~Brene Brown

I recently had to learn to trust myself again during my journey from being married for twenty years to being, well . . . not. It was by far the hardest transition I've made in my life, and I'll be forever grateful to all the family members and friends who helped along the way (you know who you are). During this time, one bright light was my amazing coach, who introduced me to a concept that many of you are likely familiar with: the idea of self-love. At first, I thought the concept was a bit strange . . . I mean, how was being loving and compassionate toward myself going to help the healing process? I clearly had a lot to learn on the subject, and what life-changing lessons they were!

First of all, I discovered the need to accept *all* of myself, including my shadow side, before I could step into a place of truly loving myself. The shadow is the side of our personality that encompasses all the parts we don't want to admit we have. There are meaningful insights that come from fully knowing and accepting oneself, including those aspects which are perceived to be dark or weak. The influential psychologist Carl Jung believed that recognizing our shadow selves was an essential step in becoming fully integrated human beings.

Once you begin a practice of self-love, you'll find over time that you lay the foundations for trusting yourself and your ability to make decisions in your own best interest. For me, it began through a process of reprogramming my belief system from seeing self-love and self-care as selfish acts to viewing them as necessary acts, ones that honor and validate my needs. This perspective was very new territory and took time and effort to sink in, but the more attuned I was to placing myself as a priority instead of an after-thought, the easier it became to do so without guilt, regret, or second-guessing. It felt like I was reclaiming parts of myself that had been hidden for far too long.

The next step on my path of exploration was a process of uncovering my core values. This experience was very enlightening, and I highly recommend it to anyone who wants to discover a way of living in closer alignment with their true selves. After tons of guided work with my coach, as well as a lot of self-reflection, I arrived at my personal list of core values, each one resonating on a deep, spiritual level. I uncovered that who I am is: kindness, faith, self-awareness, purpose, energy, and last but not least, vulnerability. Once I identified these values, I could use them as a springboard for diving deeper in my self-love practice through writing and speaking aloud daily affirmations. By declaring these statements to be true, even when I didn't completely feel it, a powerful shift was triggered in my subconscious mind. Making this part of my daily ritual has been transformative in a number of ways. It allows me to start the day with the conscious intention to raise my vibration, it helps me to be grounded in positivity, even when I'm feeling not-so-sunny (in fact, those are the days when I need my affirmations the most and find they have the greatest impact), and it provides me with a clear pathway to accessing my inner voice by being present and still in those morning moments. None of these benefits would be possible without first being vulnerable and open to learning new skills.

The truly exciting part is we *all* have this capacity within us! The opportunity to choose a higher level of self-awareness is granted with each new day. It's really up to us to decide how we make use of these extraordinary gifts.

There was a ton of inner work involved in the process of developing and trusting my intuitive skills. But I've also become keenly aware of the need to connect with others to share what I've learned. When you're on a path of expansion and growth, you tend to attract people into your life who have a similar mindset. It's like you're tuned to the same frequency, and when that happens, it's a beautiful thing.

In January 2017, after closely following a women's networking group on social media, I took a huge leap of faith and applied to open a chapter in my local area. I didn't have any formal experience in leading a women's group at the time, but I felt a strong desire to be part of what I saw unfolding online: women helping each other, lifting each other up, and bringing out their best selves in the process. People often describe the intuitive mind as a "little voice inside"—well, in this case, it was literally screaming out, "This opportunity was made for you! You have all the tools you need to succeed in this role! You can DO this!" It was hard to ignore, and I'm so glad I didn't let self-doubt take hold because it was one of the best decisions I've ever made. I posted these words in celebration of our FemCity Markham Collective's first year anniversary, and they still resonate deeply:

1. We can accomplish great things together.
2. Living in gratitude is the bomb.
3. Being around positive, passionate, and purposeful women feeds the soul.

4. "A rising tide lifts all boats." 100%!
5. Showing kindness and love can make a big difference to others. Do it.

This vibrant community wouldn't exist in my life had it not been for my intuition kicking into high gear and compelling me to act in the face of fear. When I reflect on these a-ha moments, I begin to recognize the benefits of intuition that have come over the span of many years. These gifts didn't just appear in my life magically; rather, they were acquired by grounding myself in faith (in God, others, and myself), being in a state of openness and vulnerability in order to hear the call of my inner compass, and connecting with others on this life's journey so that we can all benefit from our shared knowledge and experiences.

If I were to give a synopsis of what I've come to learn about trusting my intuition, particularly in times of stress and confusion, these would be the highlights:

1. Do regular check-ins with yourself during your day-to-day activities. Ask yourself, "How am I doing? What do I need right now?" Getting in touch with your needs in a mindful way will increase your ability to hear your inner voice.
2. Get to know yourself—the good, the bad, and everything in between. This step requires a lot of honesty and can be quite daunting at first, but it's necessary in order to step into a place of wholeness and self-compassion.
3. Find time to regularly take part in activities that resonate with you, energize you, and fill your cup. For me, self-expression through music has always provided a clear pathway to inner peace and contentment. Find whatever it is that makes your heart sing and do it often!
4. Speak life-affirming, loving, positive words to yourself. Every. Single. Day. Once mastered, it's a habit that will never cease to amaze you with its powerful influence on the intuitive mind.

"I understand now that I'm not a mess but a deeply feeling person in a messy world . . . when someone asks me why I cry so often, I say, 'For the same reason I laugh so often – because I'm paying attention.'" ~Glennon Doyle Melton

My mission in sharing my personal journey is to inspire others to see a path ahead for themselves: a path where self-doubt is replaced by self-awareness, fear is upended by courage, and feelings of unworthiness are eclipsed by feelings of empowerment. Perhaps you're experiencing barriers to self-love and self-acceptance that could be removed by learning to trust your intuition; maybe you're also going through a major transition in life and have a deep desire to access the truths that lie within you. My own experiences have taught me that entering fully into a friendship with yourself can be one of life's greatest gifts. The ongoing relationship and trust that is built from knowing yourself can also transform your other relationships for the better.

Self-awareness helped greatly during my first experiences after separation. In the past, I believed that showing vulnerability was an indicator of weakness. But as I learned to embrace this part of my personality, I found I could be more attuned to and accepting of my emotional responses in new situations instead of trying to hide them. I can now recognize the value of being in alignment with who I really am, and the innate freedom that comes with this realization. By understanding and accepting aspects of ourselves in a holistic way, we also become better equipped to discern the strengths and frailties of those around us. Wherever life's journey has taken you to this point, my sincere hope is that you will encounter a sense of security in trusting your inner guidance system and be compelled to share the light that flows from that knowledge with the world.

CHAPTER 10

LEADING FROM THE HEART

"Nothing has been more rewarding than seeing growth in others and then myself."

SHELL RICHARDSON

Shell has always had a heart for seeking and creating meaningful connections. Her passion for people has been a constant throughout her career in hospitality and event planning and through her work in the community as an active member of FemCity, Know Charlotte, and as a board member of Goodwill Industries of the Southern Piedmont. In 2015, Shell opened her business, Elegant Connexions, an event space and planning business in Concord, N.C. that connected people through hosting meaningful celebrations and meetings. She is now utilizing her passion for helping people by evolving Elegant Connexions into a business coaching service that creates relationships through community, business networking, and growth opportunities to help people realize their dreams. Such meaningful connections have now allowed Shell to realize another dream, that of becoming a published author.

www.elegantconnexions.com
ig: shell.elegantconnexions | fb: Shell Richardson
li: Shell Richardson

As a child, I always seemed to be more of a follower, probably because I was shy and timid. I would never have imagined myself as someone who would be considered a leader. However, as time grew on, I became more intrigued with goal setting and discovering my passions. I love learning, doing research, trying new things, and meeting people, and all of these things have contributed to my leadership development. I also love sharing these interests with others, whether they are members of my team or individuals I meet along the way. It makes my heart sing when I see someone reach their goals because of the training or tips I shared with them. I love the look on their faces when all the pieces begin to fall in place.

Choosing to lead has been a calling. I hate feeling like I am walking in the dark, and I appreciate having someone willing to take the time to help me to understand the "why" behind what I am doing. Remembering how I felt when I received such kindness has made me determined to do the same for others. This is what motivates me to "lead from my heart."

So with that thought in mind, I wanted to share with you some insight I have learned along the way that has helped me in my leadership journey.

WHY LEAD?

Why would anyone want to lead? I've heard some say, "I just want to do my work and go home" or "I can't be bothered; it's too much of a headache." I understand. People can be very challenging. But while being a supervisor, manager, CEO, or any other type of titled leadership role is not for everyone, you do not need to have a title to be a leader.

So what makes a good leader? What are some characteristics that would define a good or even a great leader? When I Googled this very question, I came up with quite a few answers:

1. A good leader has **clarity**. They are clear about their vision and what is needed to get things done.

2. They are **decisive**. Leaders make concrete decisions and stick to them. They are willing to do whatever it takes to see their vision through.

3. A good leader has **courage**. Some people seem to have this naturally, but for most of us, courage is something developed over time, through years of failures and disappointments. Leaders can find ways to work through these situations, using the lessons learned to build their confidence and courage for the next challenge.

4. They are **passionate** about their goals and communicate this passion to others. Ever get fired up just listening to someone else talk about something that excites them? That's how good leaders make you feel.

5. Finally, good leaders have **humility**. I want to spend a moment on this quality. Some believe humility is a weakness, but I am here to tell you that they couldn't be more wrong. Humility takes great strength. Humility understands that just because you are good at something doesn't mean you can't let someone else have the limelight.[1] A dear friend helped me to understand this when I was complaining that one of my friends didn't want to help me with a party we were hosting. She said to me, "Who typically leads in putting on these events?" I replied, "Usually, I do." She said, "Perhaps it's time to let her do something for a change, and you support her. This way, you both can take turns, and

---

1 Economy, P. (2016, March 25). The 5 Essential Qualities of a Great Leader. [Blog post]. Retrieved from https://www.inc.com/peter-economy/the-5-essential-qualities-of-a-great-leader.html

everyone is happy." I still remember her kindness in sharing this with me. Good leaders understand the impact that sharing that "moment," and even stepping aside, can have on someone else. They have a desire to see others learn, grow, and succeed. It is *not* always about them.

LEADERSHIP DEVELOPMENT TAKES TIME

Learning excellent leadership skills takes time. It is not something you develop overnight just because you came up with a good idea and decided to get the ball rolling. In this process of leading and directing others, you also have to find time to grow yourself. You will make mistakes that are seen by many, and how we react to our disappointments is all a part of the journey of leading. This is where the heart comes in. When a deep, strong desire to serve others comes from the heart, you don't have time to waste on appearances. What's important is that we realize our mistakes or errors, understand what led up to it, make a note of it, and even use it for training purposes. The goal is to avoid the same mistake in the future. This clear direction will do wonders for both yourself and those looking on.

Since most leaders are learning as they go along, there are several steps you can take to lay the groundwork for success. In *Leading from the Heart*, Jack Kahl shares some of them from his experience as a CEO and in his relationship with Sam Walton, founder of Walmart.

Yes, I know this book is about women leading. But one of the challenges women have encountered is in acquiring mentors who will help them along the way, and men can be a great resource. In addition, learning how to work with men and understanding the unique challenges that come with leading is essential to excellence. Now back to Jack Kahl!

In sharing his experience, Kahl talks about how much he learned from Sam Walton. He learned that leaders should be trustworthy, and they should be life-long learners or students. They should also be creative, driven, disciplined, and servants of their team.[2] How many people associate being an entrepreneur with serving others? Often when you hear of someone's goal of starting a business or excelling in their careers, visions of grandeur tend to accompany those dreams and goals. Reading Kahl's story impressed upon me the seriousness of leadership responsibility. It further highlighted for me that leading and assisting others should be something that comes from the heart. It is a commitment that you make to yourself to serve others. By lifting others, you will begin to soar. I have experienced this many times over.

One major step that I have taken to further my growth in my business is to create a foundation for learning. I have done this by doing what Kahl stated in his book: becoming a life-long learner. I read industry literature to improve my knowledge, take classes, attend seminars, and volunteer in my community. I have also collected a variety of mentors, which has been the most significant help of all. One of my mentors suggested that I create my own "Personal Board of Directors," and I took her advice. Some of my Personal Board members serve with me on the board at Goodwill, some are classmates, one woman is my former English professor, another is the former librarian at my university and some are personal friends. I meet with them periodically to discuss where I am in my goals, whatever challenges I happen to be facing at the moment, and any wins or improvements I have made. Such relationships have created a constant feedback loop for me and have aided me in making adjustments when necessary. They have also helped me to make difficult decisions that I otherwise would have struggled with making. Their leadership has helped me to stay focused on what's important and not become weighed down in the emotions of a situation.

My experience with my mentors leads me to my next point: it's not all about me.

---

2   Kahl, J., & Donelan, T. (2004). Leading from the heart: Choosing to be a servant leader. Westlake, OH: Jack Kahl and Associates.

IT'S NOT ABOUT ME

In 2006, I began working in the hotel industry. I loved it! I finally had a job that I felt I could sincerely enjoy, one that had growth potential but didn't have to take over my life. Every day was a learning opportunity. I was never bored, which is a good thing because I bore reasonably easily. After I had spent two years on the front desk, the executive sales director approached me about working in sales. She was considering me because one day, she approached me about a specific room that had the government rate. She wanted to know who had booked the room; I not only told who he was, but I was also able to say why he was in town. My initiative impressed her. No one had told me to get this information; it was just a habit I had to chat with people about what brought them to town. By taking this simple step, I became the sales coordinator and later the sales manager. But it didn't end there: several times we had a vacancy in the assistant general manager's position. When this happened, I would offer to help my general manager by picking up some of the work. I knew how stressful it was for him, and I had learned some of the tasks by offering to assist some of the former managers. Again, taking the initiative eventually led to my becoming the assistant general manager.

The first thing I learned when I entered the hotel is that it's not about me. My general manager had a saying, "There is no 'I' in the word team." He would continually remind us of this fact. Another adage we had is that we only want people who have a "can-do attitude." Such a person looks for ways to help the team or fill in where there is a need. Those who have a clear understanding of this quality grow to become leaders. And you want this quality to be the hallmark not only of your team but also of your leadership.

Deciding to lead is a choice. I dare say most people fall into this role or have it thrust upon them because they had the right characteristics and were hard workers. However, you eventually realize that leadership is much more than hard work: you must be willing to change your mindset. How you lead is not all about telling people what to do. Leadership is about having vision, creating a strategic plan, and communicating ideas. It's also about salesmanship: after creating, planning, and communicating, you must now sell your team on not only the vision but the belief that they have exactly what it takes to achieve it. The greater your belief and enthusiasm, the more they will believe it is possible and will help you to achieve the dream.

Of course, this mindset change must also happen in other areas of your life as well. I found this out when I had to accept a change in my life.

ACCEPT CHANGE-MINDSET

In 2013, I was diagnosed with multiple sclerosis. This diagnosis should have been a blow, but instead, it was a relief. I had suffered for years with systemic inflammation, pain, insomnia, and fatigue. I now had to figure out how to mentally adjust to this new situation. I call it my "new normal." I began to realize that to get past the diagnosis and be able to move on with my life, I had to accept my diagnosis and the challenges that came with it.

This quick adjustment in mindset was crucial because the very next year, I lost my job. Not only was I unemployed, but my husband had been laid off from his job six months earlier. The "can-do" attitude I spoke of earlier is what moved me beyond this new development to take action. With encouragement from my father, I elected to start a business. Six months later, I opened a small boutique venue that I named Elegant Connexions. This move was the beginning of a beautiful new chapter and journey that has brought me to this point.

LEADERSHIP TAKES ON NEW MEANING

My new direction began to reveal opportunities that I would not have expected. For the first time, I could chart my own course.

I could challenge myself to learn new things, take classes, and find mentors, platforms, and groups in which to participate.

What quickly became apparent to me was that I was not always comfortable in many of the settings that I found myself in. I didn't know what to do, so I decided to do nothing for the moment but keep the issue top of mind. Over time, I found information that helped me to realize I wasn't weird or unusual and that I could find another way to achieve the results that I needed. One way to do that was to create a group, so I tried forming a meet-up. I tried a couple of times and failed miserably. Then I started a women's collective called FemCity. I began to feel this was a step in the right direction.

I was used to leading in an organized setting like my corporate job, but this type of leadership presented new challenges. I have learned more about myself and grown more through FemCity than in any of my other positions. The organization has all of the things one could wish for in growth potential. In addition to creating a collective of women to attend FemCity meetings, I am able to conduct workshops, surround myself with like-minded women in business, grow both my business and myself, meet women who are already successful and are willing to share their tips . . . the list goes on. What a gold mine!

As a servant leader, I am and must be a student for life. I take this very seriously. I recognize that leadership is not about having all of the answers; it's about a willingness to fail, to make mistakes, and to grow and learn from them. This acknowledgment is one of the greatest gifts I have ever given myself. There is such freedom in understanding that I don't have to know everything.

Heart-led leadership is more about serving others than it is about making a name for yourself. It is about helping others achieve the results *they* want. True leaders do not need a title or fanfare. We cross paths with such leaders every day but may not think of them in this light. For example, I have a favorite Chinese restaurant that I love going to. Their food is excellent, but that is not why I enjoy it so much: the restaurant is family-owned, and the wife and sister of the family make me feel so welcomed every time I go there. They always ask about my parents or excitedly tell me that my parents were recently there. But the most beautiful thing the wife does whenever I am there is to ask about my business. She encourages me and tells me that I am doing a good job. She doesn't see herself as a leader, and yet she is.

My mom, sister, niece, friends, colleagues, next-door neighbor, classmates, and workmates, the majority of whom are women, have all played a role in cheering me on, giving me constructive criticism or a hug, and lending a much-needed hearing ear. They have all led without a title and most times without ever giving any thought to what they were doing. Lifting someone else is just what they do. I am in good company. All my life, I have loved the feeling that comes from assisting someone else. For me, it is far more than a calling; it is heart-led.

CHAPTER 11

THE POWER WITHIN US

*"Happiness and success will not come
to you: they will come from you"*

SALLY LOVELOCK

Sally Lovelock was born in Midland, Ontario in 1974 and moved to Burlington at the age of two. Sally attended M.M. Robinson High School-high school where she met her lifelong friends who would personify the meaning of friendship. Sally moved to England in 1995 to care for her father, who later passed away from brain cancer. While living in a small village in the country, Sally discovered the Montessori philosophy and enrolled in college at Montessori Centre International. She later went on to open her own school in 2007: Althorp Montessori School. This journey has brought Sally physical, emotional, mental, and spiritual growth. Her goal is to reach as many early year educators and parents as possible on the importance of the absorbent mind from birth to age six and how we can guide these little leaders on a path to make a big impact on our Earth.

Now living in the Niagara Region in Ontario, Canada, Sally credits her Reiki certificate for helping her find inner peace and balance while juggling her own Montessori School and two extraordinary boys.

www.althorpmontessorischool.com
ig: sally.lovelock | althorp_montessori-school

As we wake to each new day, we decide where our journey will guide us. We have a personal path to take as we climb through physical, emotional, mental, and spiritual awakenings. When we invest time in our own development, we are giving ourselves permission to be our most authentic self. There are no time limits to being who we are—it starts when we are ready.

Through my own personal journey, I have discovered that pain is in fact our greatest healer. Happiness and success will not come *to* you: they will come *from* you.

To rise as a strong, independent, successful business owner, I had to overcome many obstacles but I've learned that the importance of these obstacles is how we overcome them and use them to better ourselves. We are given only what we need to walk our future.

My first obstacle came in the form of alone time. At the age of fourteen, I broke my femur bone. I had been spoiled, growing up as the baby of four children with the consistent love of my family surrounding me. It was while I lay on my back for months that I had my first experience with alone time. I don't remember ever feeling sorry for myself; I recall just adjusting to my circumstances. Perhaps that was due to the reassurance I had from my family; they all experienced their own personal concern for their baby sister, and I worried more about them than in myself. The strength of a family unit is powerful: they were my starting foundation for building my sense of security. I realize now that this time prepared me for my future. Today I am happy in my own skin, and silence is one of my greatest healing tools.

When I was sixteen, the doctors made the decision to re-break my leg and put it in traction to lengthen it. I was ready to embrace the alone time I would spend in the hospital. My challenge this time was the physical pain: there was no medication that could ease the pain of human torture! How was this preparing me for my future?

I did eventually discover the why: it showed me I had the strength to hold back my tears as my second child came into our peaceful world. I had a C-section with an epidural that only took on one side. Thanks to my previous experience with both alone time and physical suffering, I had the mindset to overcome the pain and ensure my baby was brought into this world with a calm, present mother.

Alone time is a healthy tool that we can use to mentally prepare for our emotional journey. It gives us the opportunity to connect with our inner self and recognize that we all have the strength deep down inside to overcome our worst days. People can hold our hands and give us a shoulder, but change and healing can only come from within us. You are indeed the only person who is going to get you through your struggles.

The mental strength I had built through alone time later helped push me through two more big, life-changing events. They were those moments when you think the sun will not shine again, you can't get out of bed, and you just sink deeper and deeper. You no longer know who you are and have become completely lost. During these moments on my personal journey, I gave myself permission to grieve my loss but I knew that I needed to push through and climb to the other side.

At the age of twenty, I packed my bags and moved to England to become my father's caregiver. This was a defining moment of my process of forgiving my father for leaving me and moving to England when I was fifteen. He had three months to live, and I was going to value every minute I had with him. Through forgiveness, I knew I had the strength to be there when he needed me, and for that, he was proud.

His last words were, "Sal, I don't want you to see me this way."

The next time I saw him, he was at peace with a flower lying over his head. As the hearse pulled up outside our house and his coffin lay on display through the glass, my whole self shattered: my dad was gone. My brother Brad took my hand as we said goodbye.

It was my time to discover a spiritual world.

As I sat on the park bench in our little village in England, I needed to know my dad was still with me. I sat overlooking the green, the place where my father was born and the place where he is laid to rest. He was at peace, he was where he needed to be, and here began my time to connect with my spiritual journey.

I had the help of a lady who will never fully understand her impact on me. Wendy was the owner of the Montessori school I first worked at. She introduced me to an acupuncturist which later led me to Reiki. I found peace from her presence and in the environment she had prepared for young children, and my eyes opened to the spirit world. I was able to release the energies that took up space within me but no longer served me. This free up space in me to allow white light to flow and new positive energies to enter. I had surrendered to the universe and trusted in the plan it had for me. I found stillness in my innermost core, and I trusted myself to follow my healing journey.

Through Reiki, I found the balance I needed to start my Montessori journey and opened the doors to my own school called Althorp Montessori. Althorp is the resting place of Princess Diana, a beautiful woman I admire not for her jewels and gowns but for the overall significant effect she had in over 146 charities. When we can admire others in a healthy way, we can be truly inspired to move forward with our passions and our best self can shine.

When I opened my school, I was married to my biggest fan, the father of my amazing children. Life seemed perfect. Sadly, after years of friendship, my husband and I decided that it was time to let go of our partnership in order to show our boys what love looks like. Life was changing, and the mum guilt was real!

Not realizing I needed time to rediscover myself after my eighteen-year marriage, I moved on with life quickly. I was a strong woman, and my ego did not let me see that I was going through an identity transition. I met a man who made me believe he was the love of my life, and I gave him the best of me. It took a year for me to see that this man was truly not capable of divine love. He placed his energy into himself and would forever be the victim.

I had no chance. I was slowly losing myself to the judgments he placed on me, and sadly I became the person he saw through his eyes. I lost the power to be my authentic self. I was no longer the person I once was.

Eventually our relationship ended, and I was left wondering who I had become and how I had lost myself. My boys saw their strong, independent, self-assured mother cry inconsolably for the first time. On that day, I admitted that I was a victim, but that I knew this person could no longer define me. I had thought my answer to healing from the end of my marriage was validation from others, but my truth was within me. This second awakening to my power within built my strength and confidence, and it was so powerful that validation from others no longer mattered. This intense power inside became a force that had the ability to destroy. I had to stand back and let it simmer inside my inner core. I would hold it close until it was time to move mountains: Lang Leav calls this "rocket fuel"![1]

Through this emotional healing journey, I booked a trip to England and sat on my park bench, my happy place, overlooking the green. This was just a chapter in my story; I knew I had to challenge my inner strength and leave this chapter behind if I was going to find myself again.

This breakdown of my previous life reminded me of my inner strength and my need for alone time to rediscover my truth. However, it also taught me another important lesson on the healing journey. I learned that it is okay to ask for help and to lean on the support of your community.

I knew my children would be okay because they had a father who was ready to shine. My ex-husband was a man who loved without judgment, and he continues to be that person. We co-parent with respect for each other and respect for the needs of our children. We are a unit, just living in two different homes. We must use our intuition when choosing a partner, or any relationship in life. Is this a person who will continue to fight in your corner, is this a person who values every side of your authentic self? I made the right decision when I picked Joe as the father of my babies.

---

1   Leav, L. (2016). *The Universe of Us*. Kansas City, MO: Andrews McMeel Publishing.

I also made the right decision when it came to another incredibly important community in my life: my staff.

As the owner of a Montessori School for children from eighteen months to six years of age, I often reflect on our success. What has made our school continue to thrive and grow year after year? The answer will never change: our tribe of educators with their individual, unique skills and passion for the well-being of children in their early years. I value these relationships and the connection they share not only with me but with each other. This team of women understands the importance of inspiring one another and dropping egos as we lead young minds to a path of leadership, one child at a time.

The key to our success is understanding that this group of women have risen together and that this journey is not based solely on myself. Together they laugh, sometimes cry, but most importantly they share time together outside of work hours, allowing us to have a true understanding of who we all are. Together we encourage each other to believe in themselves and their dreams—all we ask of each other is that they be true to who they are. We invite one another to share in the success that comes from loyalty, and we offer one another the strength that comes from feeding the power that lies within us.

As I start each day in our little school, I am reminded of Maria Montessori, born August 31, 1870. Dr. Maria was Italy's first female doctor, a female leader whose words were heard back in a time when women were often not. Our school is an environment where children can connect with their inner peace. The children will flourish in this environment because it has been prepared by strong, inspiring women who are sharing the gifts of inner strength, happiness, calmness, and peacefulness through balance. Staying balanced is not easy in the hustle and bustle of modern life, but within my staff, I see a sisterhood who makes it happen! Knowing that I have a community on whom I can always rely and to whom I can turn in times of need has played a defining role in my journey of healing and awakening.

Our life's journey will take many paths, and on those paths we will come across many people who will inspire us and teach us great lessons. The people who have a great impact on our lives become pieces within us that will impact our future success. I call them "our people." They give us permission to be open to who we are and do not pass judgements. We must not build a wall around ourselves, or these people cannot cross our bridge and push us up our mountain.

Do you have that one friendship from childhood? The loyalist, the strong, non-judgmental friend who keeps it real? The person who knows all your secrets and the friend you can call at 2am? She is the friend you see in your future, holding your hand as you walk down life's road and sitting next to you in the rocking chair at the end of the journey. If you have such friendships, never let them go; their security can help ground you in your inner power. This friendship is accepting of all your imperfections and excited about your passions. With her you can shine, and without her you feel a void. Women have an amazing ability to lift one another. We must recognize that we are the woman we are today because these other strong women have been a part of our journey!

* * *

Life will bring you tragedy. You will struggle and ask yourself, "Why me?" But remember: while we cannot control what is happening, we can control how we handle it, and with that comes intense power. This is your unique personal journey, and your circumstances will help you find your inner strength. When you find that strength, and use it to inspire and build strength in others, you can conquer the world.

CHAPTER 12

LEADING FROM A PLACE OF SERVICE

"When you authentically make it about others, that's when it becomes about you."

MICHAELLA PUTMAN

Michaella Putman is a self-appointed intrapreneur with over twenty years of hands-on experience in the live event industry. Her leadership role started at thirteen years of age when she worked at a flea market snack bar. In less than a year at the ripe "old" age of fourteen, she was promoted to lead-hand, taking on a supervisory role at the concession stand. It was at that point that Michaella started to become aware of the meaning behind the guest experience on both sides of the concession stand.

Later while studying at Ryerson University, Michaella became acutely aware of the impact the guest experience had not only in the sales cycle but also in the psyche of staff.

That knowledge, combined with the opportunity to work with some of the preeminent professional sports organizations, promoters, and venue management organizations in the world, has shaped how Michaella builds teams in the live event industry.

In the end, Michaella wants to do things that haven't been done before for people, partners, and organizations. She aims to drive the fan experience and team development from a place of authenticity and service. She is here to make magic for herself, her family, and those around her.

li: michaellaputman

"Michaella:

- is a cheerful little girl who is eager for new tasks and experiences;
- plays well with other children and adjusts well to new situations;
- can complete a task with minimum need for supervision and shows creativity in the use of art materials."

My leadership path and style started when I was very young. The above comments came from my junior kindergarten report card; it is funny to me that I am still that girl so many years later and in so many ways. My mom recently told me a story about dropping me off at nursery school; I would cling to the door and have a meltdown as she left for work. But with time, and as it is for many kids, when it came time to pick me up from nursery school, my mom found me helping out, tidying up, sweeping the floor, and assisting the other children. Being of service to others always made me happy.

Helping has been a constant theme in my life. But who could have known back then how being the teacher's helper would chart the course to what I would become to myself and others?

So there I was, a happy-go-lucky, helpful, creative girl who by grade eight graduation wanted to be a fashion designer. By high school, those dreams had started to come true as I relished every moment of home economics class: making clothes for myself and my friends, making tops and selling them to my English teacher, and the piece de resistance, making two prom dresses. The dresses themselves were straight out of the '80s and early '90s with big shoulder pads and tapered skirts. The fabric was luxurious velveteen straight out of an episode of the '80s classic *Dynasty*. When a friend of mine wore one of my hand-crafted prom dresses to see a theatre show, she was stopped by a woman in the bathroom who told her she loved the dress. With that news, I felt like I had *arrived!* Making and selling clothes satisfied my need to be creative, help others feel good, and solve a problem—all of which also made me money.

This need to help others feel good, which happened to generate revenue as a result, revealed itself again when I was in university. I had the opportunity to work with my father at his high-end restaurant. It was a great job that allowed me to make money to cover the expenses that came with being a student. It also continued to make me acutely aware of the need to pay attention to the small and essential details. You see, the restaurant was private, meaning it would typically be the same guests coming in daily. I watched my father memorize the details of each member's family and business, where they like to sit, and what they enjoyed from the menu. He paid attention to it all. It was not about him; it was about his guests. And it was not only about the guests in the restaurant; more importantly, it was also about the guests behind the scenes: the staff.

The staff were addressed by Mr. or Ms. and their first name. It was a sign of respect that the team earned and deserved, even when something or situations did not go as planned. My father's ability to pay attention to both the guests and the staff, to go above and beyond for others before himself, once again reinforced how I would lead in the future.

Taking what I learned from my father and applying it at university proved fruitful. I was part of a group presentation before the Christmas break in which our team had to "pitch" to a company looking to hold a destination meeting for their top restaurant managers. Aside from the information we were presenting, we also focused heavily on "setting the scene" for the presentation (aka the reveal), which was taking place in a classroom. I purchased fabric to mimic tablecloths and spent all night making centerpieces for the tables: topiary trees, which were a popular home decor item at the time. Wanting to amp up the reveal, I decided that since it was the holidays, I would use "holiday" scented potpourri that smelled of pine or cinnamon to help evoke the scent and sense of Christmas. The presentation went well, and as we were cleaning up, the professor asked me how much I would sell the centrepieces for. When I responded that I didn't know, he asked me how much I had spent making the pieces. "Ten dollars, I think," I said. His response: "But how much time did you spend making the pieces? You need to take that into account." I responded that it had taken me a couple of hours.

Our professor said he would take all four of them for twenty dollars each. He then handed me a bit more than the eighty dollars he owed and said, "Keep the change."

I realized once again that going above and beyond, paying attention to the small details, and providing a service-based solution had allowed my professor to get some of his Christmas shopping done. It had also allowed me to generate revenue and assisted in helping our group to receive a favorable grade.

Why am I telling you all these stories? Because as I look back at my life story thus far, no matter what projects, positions, or passions I have had, there has been the theme of service—making it about others. It has become the foundation of my leadership style.

Leading in this style has been the backbone of some of my greatest successes and recognition. But more importantly, some of those same experiences have allowed me to have some of my most essential failures (otherwise known as opportunities).

Developing my leadership style with a service-oriented foundation has at times led to burn out, overthinking, a want to please all, and a fear of not being liked, which often did not work to my benefit (I don't think it would work to anyone's advantage). It could be paralyzing at times. Leadership became more about the voice of others rather than my own. In my mind, I always needed to retain the image of being "a cheerful little girl who is eager for new tasks and experiences, the "yes girl," the girl who undoubtedly knew that the guest was always right.

The first time I experienced this in my leadership style was in my position as manager of guest service at an arena. It was a brand new venue, and the marquee venue for the city. My job was to be the voice of the guests. It was a proactive service position, which at the time was a new concept in the world of guest service. Although my role and the role of the guest services team was to assist guests with everything from lost and found items to seat issues, the position also required me to look to the future of all the venue's various events and anticipate potential problems. We would then make adjustments as much as we could to prevent issues or be ready on the spot with some solutions and future follow-up with the fans. It was the perfect role for this "service-oriented people pleaser."

The most amazing part was that there was no blueprint: the team and I, with the support of management, developed how situations would or should be handled. We welcomed guests with open arms, ready to create a great experience and make magic. Even on the nights when things didn't go as planned and guests shared their frustration, we remained positive. We focused on solutions to make them happy based on the premise that the guest was always right and their perception was their reality.

As one could imagine, working at a busy venue with a multitude of events and hundreds of thousands of fans coming through its doors and managing our fair share of concerns over time led to a change in my personality. The guest service desks and the department became a dumping ground at times for guests' concerns that did not start at the venue but ended up there. Some nights it was hard to remain positive not only for myself but for the team. I was struggling with the premise that the guest was always right because my gut started to tell me that was not always the case. But although my gut was telling me something, the fear of going against the grain of what I thought needed to be cheery, peppy, positive, and full of jazz hands all the time loomed in my head. Sometimes I felt physically ill in this role; I would take on the emotions and frustrations of the guests and of our team as I tried to please them as best as I could.

I don't remember when it started or even how it started, but over time I began to listen to my gut over my head; we as a department began to shift away from the golden rule that the guest was always right to an updated golden rule that the guest was not always correct. We actively listened to their concern, empathized with them, and made sure they felt that they had been heard, but there would not be free tickets to an upcoming event or a full refund as the solution for every concern. Sometimes this solution worked, as they only wanted to have someone listen. However, there were times when that solution didn't work; at those times, it was hard for me to move through the situation. My natural instinct was to want to please the guest no matter what; however, my gut told me the new way of handling things was right.

We started to hold the guest accountable for their actions, and I felt this put less stress on our team. For example, if a fan sat in their seat for the entire night not being happy that people around them were dancing but decided to say nothing to event staff for the whole evening, and then came by our desk looking for a refund or tickets to another event—we declined that solution. We would instead let them know that had they brought this up to a staff member as soon as it became a concern, we could have found options to relocate them or work toward another solution; however, since the show had come and gone, there was nothing we could do and they should next time bring it to our attention sooner so we could work together to find a solution.

Even as I type this out now, it still feels a bit against my grain, as it doesn't feel very service-oriented. However, as time has gone on, it has started to feel more right; much like filling another's cup before filling your own can be detrimental, I have come to believe that you have to find a balance between being of service and "over-serving." By starting to learn and lead in this manner, I not only regained my sanity, but I believe I helped our guest services team as a whole. We started to trust the process if even it meant we could not make every guest happy (and we tried!). I feel it also connected us as a team because we had each other's backs.

I have held many roles since that guest service role, but no matter the title, I have found myself naturally leading from a place of service and making it about others; this has allowed me to experience success at all levels, personally, professionally, and financially. I am still very much the "cheerful little girl who is eager for new tasks and experiences." I believe that everything matters and that it truly is the small things that make the most significant impact. That being said, I am much more aware that everything matters at different levels. Now if I find myself "over-serving," I rewrite or adjust the rules, I line up what matters most in the moment (which may be me taking a step back and not do anything for a brief time), and then I work through the small things and watch the magic happen!

CHAPTER 13

FINDING MAGIC THROUGH FEAR AND FAILURE

"You need to trust that the magic inside of you is greater than any fear."

ELIZABETH MEEKES

Elizabeth Meekes is a coach, holistic practitioner, writer, podcaster, speaker, entrepreneur, and eternal student of the Universe. She completed a bachelor of arts at Wilfrid Laurier University where she found her passion in radio and was recognized for her work with Radio Laurier.

As a holistic practitioner, Elizabeth is passionate about health and wellness. When it felt as if her love of learning was missing from her life and business, this inner calling pushed her to become a certified life coach through the Centre for Applied Neuroscience. Elizabeth is committed to consistent growth and learning and believes that the greatest investment we can make is in ourselves. Following that commitment, she continues to learn from her own mentors/coaches, who have included Gabby Bernstein, Anne Beauvais, and Harriette Hale.

Elizabeth is passion, determination, strength, and love. She is a spiritual gangster: deeply connected to the power of the Universe. Her mission is to create massive change in this world through being raw and true in her power, standing back up every time she falls, and empowering you to do the same. She shares this incredible life with her partner Steve and their two boys, Rowan and Arion.

www.elizabethmeekes.com
ig: @lizmeekes | fb: @lizmeekes

I sat on the side of the tub with my face in my hands, waiting for the ding of the three-minute timer. Let's be honest: I couldn't wait three minutes for this. After what must have been less than a minute, I looked down at the test.

Pregnant.

3+ weeks.

Shit.

It was February. I had graduated university in the spring of the previous year and was now spending my time managing the Mc-Donald's I had worked at since high school, freelancing part time as a make-up artist, and continuing to work for the university radio station. I had no idea what I wanted out of my life. Honestly, I think I was waiting and hoping it would just happen for me—you know, passively sitting around waiting for all my dreams to come true, not actually knowing what any of those dreams were. Isn't that how this shit works?

Retrospect: No . . . it is most definitely *not* how it works.

That moment in the bathroom of my parents' house is when it all started to shift. I was like, *"Okay Universe, I hear you. Challenge accepted." Of course,* I did not have this clarity then, but now looking back on my journey, that was the first time I did not hide from uncertainty. I moved forward, accepting the invitation from the Universe to step into myself fully and learn my purpose. Passive wouldn't work for me anymore. I thought, *"All* right Universe, let's try it your way."

Before I get ahead of myself, I will note that I believe spirituality is unique to each of us. I connect with the Universe, but please each time you read those words, sub in anything from your own belief and understanding, such as God, Source, Love, etc.

Now this wasn't your typical business deal, my agreement with the Universe, as if it ever is with Her. As the Universe would have it, our handshake came in the form of a rush of uncontrollable emotion with not much thought attached. I was sobbing and struggling to catch my breath. If you ever have the honor of connecting with my sister, ask her about the distraught phone call she received that day right before I raced to her work to deliver the news. Despite my overwhelming fear and anxiety, though, there wasn't a doubt in my mind: I knew I would have this baby. Although in the spirit of true honesty, he was not often referred to as baby until he came into the physical world; instead I nicknamed him my little alien. Baby was hard for me. Truly, the whole thing was hard for me. I had planned for a life with no children, and now here I was undoubtedly having one.

There is a reason this pregnancy shook me to my core and opened me up to something so much greater than me. My partner and I were careful. If there were to have been an oops in any of my relations, statistically this was not the time for it to happen. It should have certainly been years earlier when I used my body without much thought for the potential consequences. By the time I learned I was pregnant, I had developed some self-respect and had been doing what was in my power to protect my body. This in and of itself told me that there was something more here. I knew there was a purpose for the pregnancy happening at that given time, and I trusted it as a sign of something much bigger than me at work. I now refer to that power as *the Universe*.

WHAT DO YOU BELIEVE?

One of my biggest fears about having children, and one of the greatest reasons I did not include them in my original life plan, was this: I believed that being a mom meant I was only a mom. I thought that I would be completely lost in motherhood, and there would be no space for me anymore. It's ironic really, because I had no idea who she was, that person I did not want to lose in motherhood, until I dove in head first and pushed myself to dig deeper to find her. So in fact, I did not lose myself in motherhood at all. Rather, I opened myself up deeply, I became committed to myself and my growth so that I could raise awesome humans to the best of my ability, and for the first time, I met my true *self*. I didn't recognize how limiting my belief about motherhood was until I was so afraid of it being true that I did the work to prove to myself it wasn't.

I also believed that I wasn't enough, for anything really. I didn't pursue any dreams that I may have had because I thought rejection was inevitable. Even more so, I was terrified of not being rejected; I truly believed that if anyone actually fed into my dreams, they would be seriously misguided because there was absolutely no way I was worthy of that "shit," nor would I be any good at it. I didn't believe I had a voice worth sharing. I did not think I was worthy.

Sound familiar? I ask because this is a common one. So let me make something very clear. You are not weak. You are not small. You have a voice to share with the world. And you have the power to do it. You are so fucking worthy. I am saying this to all of you out there, especially those of you shaking your head thinking, *"No, not me."* Yes, Love, YOU.

Before we can shift, we need to know where we are shifting from. Let's start with an inventory of your self-limiting beliefs. Grab a pen and paper and spend the next five minutes free writing. What do you believe about yourself, about other people, about life? Are those beliefs serving you?

LETTING GO

Now take those limiting beliefs,and let that shit go. Recognize that it is no longer serving you. It's important to understand that these beliefs have been programmed into us throughout our lives, so it's safe to say it will take a little more than stating you have let it go for them to actually take the hint and go. So start here: create an awareness around the stories you are telling yourself. If you completed the belief inventory exercise, you've already begun doing this.

The next step is to acknowledge when that stuff is coming up for you and take note of how it is impacting your life. As I write this, the voice of the ego has crept back in, whispering, *"You are not enough, who are you to write this, what do you possibly have to say?"* Remember: this shit has been programmed. We are human. Even once we have let it go, it will sneak back in from time to time. The difference is, once you have created that awareness and shifted your mindset, you can see those old beliefs for what they are, and you can choose differently.

It's also time to let go of that which you can't control. Every single thing. Expectations included. Others' ideas of who and what and how you should be are none of your business. Their judgement is merely a reflection of their perception. It does not matter. You find what you love, and you do you, Love. Let go of this idea that you need to be in any way other than how you are. The world doesn't need more people in masks: it needs more people shining their light, standing in truth, power and love.

TAKE CONTROL

Maybe this sounds a little counter-intuitive after all that advice about letting go. I promise you, it's not. Get to know the *one thing* you can control: yourself—mind, body, and soul. Own your shit. Take responsibility for your judgements, expectations, and fears. Recognize the power of your thoughts. You are a co-creator of your reality through your perception, what you think, and what you feel. How do you perceive the world around you? How are you feeding your mind, body, and soul?

We decide what this life looks like for us. That was a hard pill for me to swallow. You see, when you are passively letting life happen *to* you, as I was, rather than choosing to have life happen *for* you, it's easy to play the blame game. But it's also really lonely and unfulfilling. It is so much more powerful to take responsibility and actively design the life you want. I will always choose the discomfort of growth over the discomfort of sitting in stagnant water. Taking control means taking a serious look at what you are consuming. How much time are you spending scrolling social media or watching TV? What are you putting into your body? How much time do you spend in nature? How often do you move your body? Now what would it look like to consciously feed your mind, body, and soul every single day?

Imagine you are living your dream life right now. How does that version of you show up for herself every day? Start showing up like her. If you really want that life, if you want to make that shift, you need to start showing up as the you who is on the other side of it. Because all of that is inside you already. It is not your outer circumstances that determine how much of a badass you are. That's all you, Love.

BE AFRAID AND DO IT ANYWAY

Lean into fear. You have two options: sit still or move. If you're anything like me, it's a no brainer: you chose the latter. But to move, you need to stare straight down the barrel of fear. You need to trust that the magic inside of you is greater than any fear. You can even take it one step further and use that fear as a roadmap to guide you. Recognize when something is both scary and exciting, when you're terrified yet amazed and inspired by what lies on the other side of that fear.

When I began studying as a holistic practitioner, I was terrified. We didn't have money to go to a pumpkin patch at Halloween, let alone for me to invest in any courses. I had one baby at home and another on their way, and I had no idea if pursuing this as a career would even work. But what was even greater than my fear was my excitement and that magnetic pull inside me that said this is what I was meant to do next. If we had more time here, I would dive into intuition, but for now I will tell you this: when you have that feeling, that magnetic pull, that unexplainable knowing that may contradict all logic and reason, trust it.

FALL DOWN SEVEN TIMES, STAND UP EIGHT

There is a Japanese proverb that translates to: pushing us to keep going, no matter what, to keep moving forward. Get yourself comfortable with failure.

Listen, I had one plan for my life: no children. My plan failed. If I can fail on such a life-altering scale, if I can allow that failure to catapult me into a spiritual awakening in which I learn every day to trust in the Universe and come back to my truth and my power, to get back up every time I fall, you can, too. When our plans fail, big or small, it is often because the Universe has something much greater in store for us. I am so damn grateful the Universe had a plan for me that opened me up to step into my purpose. My plan failing was the greatest shift in my life. Accepting the invitation to learn and grow through all the assignments that shift has included thus far has allowed me to acknowledge the woman I am, and embrace her fully.

You are on this earth in this body for a reason. You are worthy of following your dreams. And when you fall (because you will), you have the strength in you to accept the challenge, take the lesson, and get the hell back up.

Teach yourself to stand back up every time you fall. If you are serious about making a shift in your life, finding your purpose, and stepping into your power, there will be times when things don't work out exactly as you have planned. And if I am being honest, that's a good thing. We learn much more from our failures than we do from our successes. That's where the lessons are. If you're completely resisting this idea, keep reading. The last piece I have for you will hopefully take a little of the fear out of the fall.

FIND YOUR PEOPLE

Where are your people? Where are the people who have been through it and made it to the other side stronger and wiser? Where are the people who can see your magic and support you as you allow it to shine? Where are the people who are committed to growth, to being afraid and doing it anyways? Where are *your* people?

For when you fall, and when you rise, find your people. The people who have been where you have been. The people who have done the work and continue to do the work, who have failed and stood back up, who are committed to owning their truth. It's a hell of a lot easier to do something scary when you have your people there to support you through it.

From the day I started studying to be a holistic practitioner, to the day I started my life coach training, and still to this day, I am never without a mentor or a coach. I surround myself with people who will support my journey and push me to continue growing into the best version of me.

Surround yourself with people who inspire you.

FIND YOUR MAGIC

To the women who find a little of themselves in my story, I share this for you. I was a woman passively riding the waves of life (and by riding, naturally I mean being slammed again and again down to the ocean floor with no life vest in sight). I see her and I feel her, that girl struggling for air. I am so damn grateful for her because without her, I wouldn't be the woman who has stepped into the light and created a life that I am excited about, while leading other women like you to do the same. I've found my magic and it's so fucking beautiful. It is my soul's purpose to guide you to yours. I know you have it, too. There is so much magic inside you, and you are worthy of every drop of it. It's time to give yourself that. Your soul has been crying out for it.

It's time to find your magic. Let's rise.

143

CHAPTER 14

LIFE IS SHORT. BE TRUE TO WHO YOU ARE AND WHAT YOU WANT

*"Be brave enough to listen to your
gut, make your own rules, and create
a life that is your own version of
having it all."*

JULIA LEFAIVRE

Julia is a powerhouse. This multi-business owner and mom of three isn't going to use her kids as an excuse not to follow her dreams of making an impact in this world. In fact, her children are her reason.

Julia was an elementary school teacher for almost ten years. When her second child was born, she felt like she needed a change. She began an online fitness business while teaching full time and managing two little ones. Some might say she is crazy! But she truly has a passion for wanting to make an impact in the lives of women.

A couple years into her business, Julia decided to leave her teaching career to pursue her business full time. It has since grown into a five-star podcast, *The Thriving Woman*, as well as coaching and mentoring women in business. She uses her personal experiences and passion to help guide women to continue to adventure and dream big even after becoming a mom.

https://julialefaivre.mykajabi.com
ig: @julialefaivre | fb: @JuliaLefaivreCoach

The summer before my senior year of high school, our family received some news that forever changed my life. My cousin's cancer had spread and she was given only a few months to live. She was four years old.

I was sitting in my senior English class when the classroom phone rang. My heart sank, and then I was called out of the classroom. *Did she pass? Was this it?* I felt like I was going to throw up. As I sat down in the counsellor's office, I could feel my heart racing, my palms sweating. and the tears welling up in my eyes. The counsellor started to speak. "So have you decided where you are going to apply next year?" *Wait. What?*

It wasn't until four months later on New Year's Eve that my cousin took her last breath here on Earth. We had been visiting my aunt and uncle for the holidays, trying to create some sense of normalcy amidst the grim reality of her diagnosis. My father, brother, and I had left the day prior because I had a shift at our local department store in our hometown two hours away. That night when I came home from my shift, I sat in the living room, trying to get the TV set up to watch the New Year's Eve celebrations happening across the country, when my dad called from the kitchen, "Emily passed away this afternoon."

My heart sank. My friends changed their plans and came to spend that evening with me so I would not be alone as I came to terms with the fact that my little cousin was gone. Searching my memory bank for a sense of connection, I recalled a conversation I had with her that summer, just before she became sick. We were playing in her backyard and hanging out on the swings.

She had turned to me and asked, "Do you love yourself?"

Gosh, what kind of four-year-old asks that?

"Yes, of course I do!"

I'm not sure I completely believed my answer at the time but thought it was the best response. *Just say yes so she will, too!*

Emily's death hit me hard, and I spent my senior year different from most of my peers. I moved in a state of shock, this total out-of-body experience. Like I was watching my life but wasn't really living it. But ultimately Emily's death taught me two things: 1) life is short and 2) love who you are and share your gifts with the world.

And so I began to give myself permission to be me and to live life on my own terms. I used to be that girl who followed all the rules. The kids in school called me "goody two shoes" or "brown noser." I wanted to please everyone, make sure that everyone was happy and that conflict was far enough away for everyone to be comfortable. But the death of my cousin, as well as a few other big life moments, brought me to my knees and showed me a few things. They taught me that some rules are meant to be broken because the rules that society or our parents created for our future are merely opinions and suggestions. They also taught me that discovering who I am and what I wanted for my life needed to become my priority.

Have you ever decided to give up on a dream because the mountain seemed too steep to climb? Many of us believe that our path should be linear, but it is not. Our journeys are windy with many obstacles that get in our way. We are all given mountains to climb. I have climbed many mountains in my own life, and not just the ones in the Canadian Rockies where I have lived for the past thirteen years. But we all have the power to rise up, climb that mountain, and experience the bliss and joy the summit has to offer.

I was chatting with a friend recently with whom I had shared my journey of loss and growth and she responded with, "Wow! You are brave!"

I have never heard anyone describe me that way, nor would I describe myself as brave. But I guess if trusting your intuition and following your heart equates to being brave then yes! I am brave!

I have learned to lean into the fears, overcome my need to please and meet the expectations of others, listen to my intuition, and ultimately find a life of gratitude, joy, and fulfillment.

As a young adult, I thought that I was supposed to be Emily's teacher,but truly she was teaching me a lesson. To love myself. To be me! In death, we are always given a gift. It is up to us to realize and be open to receiving it. It has taken me many years to listen, but now I hear her loud and clear. She taught me that we are only given one life to live. It doesn't matter *how long* we are here: what matters is what we *do* with our time here. She was only given five years but boy, did she ever make a huge impact. She taught me that I am here to share my story and experiences to continue to make the impact on others that she made on me. She taught me that I have a responsibility to live my life with intention and alignment with who I want to be.

After Emily's death, I had to start paying attention and figure out what I really wanted in life. With some courage, I began making decisions based on what I wanted and how I wanted to feel, which is a right and freedom that we all have access to but that we sadly underutilize. As I became an adult and headed off to university, I entered the years that would be some of my most profound experiences of trial, exploration, and self-discovery. We often think that discovery is a perfect process, but I can tell you it wasn't that way for me. I made many mistakes, failed, and failed again, but those struggles, those *mountains* are what made me who I am today.

My decisions started to become more bold, including things that I had always wanted to do and try. I seized an opportunity to live and work on a cruise ship for six months between completing my bachelor degree and getting my master degree in teaching. I lived for a year and a half in Australia as part of my studies for my teaching degree. Many other people still remembered me as the girl who followed all of the rules, and so the decisions I began making for me often seemed uncharacteristic and rebellious to them.

A year into my teaching career, I met my husband. What began as a summer fling . . . Okay, I will be honest: I was in love with him the moment I met him. We hung out the entire summer, after which

I was set to return for my second year of teaching while he had been offered a job in Western Canada, three thousand kilometers away. We decided to do the long-distance relationship thing but only made it nine months before we were both trying to figure out how one of us could relocate. If he left Alberta, he would not have a job to come home to in Ontario, so we decided that I would move west because I could teach anywhere in Canada. However, I had to decide whether to finish out the school year where I was or take a leap of faith and trust that all would work itself out. In a moment of bravery, I quit my teaching job and on April 19, 2007, I moved west.

I had little support. People asked, "What are you thinking? Just finish off the school year." I remember a friend bursting into tears when I told her the news. I even had another friend go as far as to say, "But *when* you break up, you are too far away for me to help." All everyone saw was a rash decision and failure, but their perceptions and reactions were based on fear and logic, whereas mine were based on joy, intuition, and knowing exactly what I wanted for my life. We won't always have the support of those closest to us, but that is not a sign to stop listening to your intuition. Screw logic—listen to what your heart wants! Trust your gut! At the end of the day, it is not our job to make anyone happy but ourselves. If there are people in our lives who don't support our goals, it doesn't mean that they don't support *us*. They are showing that they care, just in a different way than we may expect or desire. It could also be that our vision is not clear to them, even though it is often so clear and simple to us. Have compassion for those who may not initially show their support, but also know that it is not up to anyone else to believe in your dreams and vision. That's your job first. As N.R. Narayana Murthy said, "*Growth is painful. Change is painful. But, nothing is as painful as staying stuck where you do not belong.*"

* * *

That place of unbelonging may be a physical location or a state of mind. For me, it was both!

Eight years ago, I found myself staring up at another mountain. When my first child was only two months old and while I was still on maternity leave, I was laid off from my teaching career due to cutbacks. Looking back now, I see that the Universe had been giving me signs all along. My intuition and gut told me it was time for something new, but I fought it. How could I leave a career I had known for so long? I fought hard to get back to teaching. I went back to work when my son was ten months old and then again when my daughter, our second child, was only nine months old. The thing is, when we resist what the Universe is trying to tell us, life can become hard. Whereas when we stop resisting and listen to our gut, life can feel so simple, easy, and in flow.

As of five years ago, I was still fighting that inner voice. I was teaching full time, a mom of two little ones, and building a health coaching and mentoring business on the side. I still had no intention of ever leaving my career as a teacher, but things slowly started to shift.

It all finally caught up to me when my children were ages two and three and I landed myself on a stress leave from work. The stress leave provided me with a lot of time to reflect on who I was as a wife, a mother, and a woman. I loved teaching but it no longer fulfilled me and was no longer aligned with what I wanted. I had evolved, and my needs and wants had started to evolve, too. For so many years, I had been so good at knowing who I was and making aligned decisions, but when I became a mom, I had inadvertently put my own alignment aside. We hear this so often from new moms: "Who Am I now?" we tend to lose ourselves as we take on the powerful role of parenthood. It took a stress leave to recenter myself and be honest with who I was and what I wanted for my life and for my young family.

My leave was not welcomed by my employer; in fact, it came with threats and bullying and ended with a fight with the union. I was advised of the potential consequences of that fight but was also told I would win. I knew that I had to rise up at that moment. I knew that me fighting the school board was not about me or about the wages they withheld illegally—it was about fighting for every past, present, and future employee. So I fought, and I won!

On June 28, 2015, I enjoyed my last day of teaching and said farewell to a career I had known for ten years. Just like that. I wanted a career, but I also wanted less stress, more time, more flexibility. Was it scary? Hell yes! Was I making a teaching salary in my online business? Hell no! Was it worth it? One thousand times yes, because when we truly align our actions and our goals with who we are and what we want, it will lead us to a life of gratitude, joy, and fulfillment. Leaving my career gave me all the things that I was so desperately wanting. I was less stressed, I had more time with my family and more time to do the things I loved, and I had the flexibility to create my day-to-day life on my terms.

It has been five years since I listened to my intuition to leave my teaching career to pursue my business full time. My husband and I have since welcomed our third child and my business continues to grow. Listening to my gut has opened my eyes to be more present to life and the Universe. It's enabled me to be present with our children, being there for every minute and every milestone. It has allowed me to be more present in my business, which has in turn allowed me to give more to my clients and make a bigger impact supporting women who want more for their lives. It has brought even more opportunity into our lives.

In death, Emily's message to me was to love myself, love who I was, and align who I was with what I want. It is now my responsibility to share that message with others. We don't need to settle for a life lived in the priorities of anyone but ourselves.

I now guide and support others in achieving their goals and aspirations both in business and in life. I give them the tools to listen to their gut and follow their instinct to align with who they truly are and achieve what they want for their life.

I often find myself being asked if I will ever return to teaching. The truth is I never left. I may have left the education system, but I remain true to my gifts: to teach, to empower, and to help others tap into their true potential. Only now, my classroom is much larger with a different population of students.

Here is what I know for sure. I was put on this Earth to experience loss, pain, and challenges so that I could discover my own strength. It is through that determination, perseverance, and strength that I am able to RISE UP and share my message with other women to show them that they can, too. Since my cousin's passing over twenty years ago, I have worked on myself, growing and evolving into the woman I am today. I have been given many mountains in my life, not just to challenge myself but to show me just how strong I am so that we can climb those mountains together.

So we must ask ourselves: do we want to come to the end of life and regret the chances we didn't take? Or do we want to know that we truly lived this life with one hundred percent authenticity in who we are and what we wanted?

WORLD

LEAD AS WOMEN
TOGETHER

CHAPTER 15

GIRL GANG

*"Mean girls run cliques. Empowered
women build girl gangs!"*

JESSICA KHOURI

Jessica is an event specialist, digital marketer, and writer. She is the co-owner of Paperback Events and the Co-Founder of the MilSpouse Collective, a professional and social network for Canadian military spouses. Her passion lies in planning events that empower women and in creating positive social change through feminist community building. Jessica is a mom to one, a dog mom to two, and a fierce supporter of girl gangs everywhere.

www.jesskhouri.com | www.paperbackevents.com
ig: @paperbackevents | @jessicamkhouri | fb: @Paperback Events
li: Jessica Khouri | T: @writewithjessk

"Starting a girl gang of women aggressively supporting other women so hands up if you want in because if we get enough people, we're totally getting jackets." ~@teamBossBabe

Um. We totally got jackets. In April of 2019, I organized an event. A girl gang event. Fourteen women came, drank rosé, and made their own "girl gang" jackets. In doing so, we unofficially started a girl gang. A community of support. A cheerleading section. A group of women who silently yet unwaveringly decided that competition was so passe.

I'm here for collabs. I'm here for ladies cheering on ladies. As women, we stand a better chance of leading and succeeding by building a foundation of support rather than a structure of competition. I'm a firm believer that you need a girl gang to level up and that you need a squad to make you a better leader. We need to cheer on other women, even when the world is telling us not to. Girl gangs are in. And they're here to stay.

WHY GIRL GANGS? WHY NOW?

When 2019 kicked off, I was filled with optimism and drive, the kind that only comes from a fresh new year. With resolutions made to the sound of champagne popping, I swore to make this the best year ever. More specifically, I was resolved to be the cheerleader I needed. 2019 was going to be the year I embraced and celebrated other women in business and the year I was going to find power in collaboration. Seriously, I was over the adult world of "mean

159

girls," or rather the idea that we still need to embody the mean girl stereotype.

Girls are socialized from a young age to be in competition with each other. Schoolyard comparisons are both precursors to and fuel for a mean girl mentality. According to Kellie Sanders, " . . . *negative interactions between girls have been dismissed for years by many as normal rites of passage.*"[1] We're taught to believe that being mean to each other, that wearing our mean girl mask, is normal. Mean girl culture is normalized, and by the time we reach high school, this culture has reached its peak of mean. I'm talking Regina George levels of mean. "You can't sit with us" levels of mean.[2]

The reality is, this culture supports and is supported by a patriarchal society. Mean girl culture perpetuates the idea that we're each other's biggest competition and prevents us from being allies.[3] As women, we have enough obstacles to navigate and overcome within a world that operates on gender-based power relations. We need to overcome the mean girl stereotype and start normalizing a girl gang culture instead.

Theoretically, mean girl culture should have ended in high school. And yet I find myself, thirty-one years old and an entrepreneur of three years, still engulfed in, and sometimes guilty of, a world of mean girls and competition. "You can't sit with us" has become "you can't work with us, you can't create with us, you can't launch with us," etc. There's this belief that there's not enough room for all of us at the top. That someone else's success necessarily means a lack of success for us. This fuels self-doubt, criticism, and competition. Or at least it did for me.

I see stories of other women's success on Instagram and I know I should be happy for them. But is this what I truly feel? Not al-

1   Sanders, Kelly. (2015) "Mean Girls, Homosociality, and Football: an education on social and power dynamics between girls and women." *Gender and Education, Vol. 27.* (Issue 7). Pg. 887-908.
2   Messick, Jill (Executive Producer), & Waters, Mark (Director). (2004). *Mean Girls* [Motion Picture]. USA: Paramount Pictures.
3   Weiss, Suzannah. (2016, June 27). 5 Reasons The Catty Woman Trope Has Got To Go, Because It's Fueling The Patriarchy. Retrieved from https://www.bustle.com/articles/169376-5-reasons-the-catty-woman-trope-has-got-to-go-because-its-fueling-the-patriarchy

ways! Sometimes my gut reaction is jealousy and I run an internal dialogue of "why not me?". It's too easy to fall into a cycle of comparing every aspect of your life or your business to other women.

I'm not saying that a little competition doesn't serve a purpose, but too much fixation on it can leave you in a negative and unproductive place. Minutes become hours of missed work when you're focusing on someone else. Seriously, it's really unproductive. As a business owner, I often find myself looking at similar businesses, studying what they're doing and how they're doing. I sometimes find myself balancing on a thin line between market research and comparison/competition. The latter can be so problematic for so many reasons. Not only has checking my social media feeds become an obsession for me, but constantly worrying about someone else's game only hurts my own business. My ability to think, work, and create has been obstructed by feelings of jealousy and anger. These kinds of actions and feelings only feed and grow the adult world of mean girls. The reality is, there is space for all of us in the winner's circle. There is so much room for all of us to succeed, and we can throw a girl gang party and celebrate each other while we're there.

GIRL GANGS BUILD LEADERS

In all honesty, I would not be where I am today without other women. When I first started my business, Paperback Events, I was supported and encouraged by other local women. My business partner and I were lucky to be able to network and collaborate with other businesswomen. Whether it was liking or sharing our posts on social media, attending our events, or partnering with us on projects, we were and continue to be lucky to be surrounded by so many supportive women. We unofficially had a girl gang, and I can't thank them enough.

As women in business, we already face a number of obstacles; we don't need to also be obstacles for each other. More than that, we need to create and cultivate community, because entrepreneurship can be really lonely and isolating. Our success is and should be collaborative.

The women leaders we see and look up to have a group of other women behind them shouting, "Yes girl!". Lauren Graham, aka Lorelie Gilmore, said, "Let's keep lifting each other up. It's not lost on me that two of the biggest opportunities I've had to break into the next level were given to me by successful women in positions of power."[4] We have to lead by supporting other women, by collaboratively leveling up and celebrating success together. So how do you build your girl gang?

1. S-U-P-P-O-R-T. Support!

This one seems pretty obvious, but I have to tell you, it's hard for some people. Because I'm not talking surface-level support. I'm talking genuine, authentic support, support-you-even-if-no-one's-watching support. It's easy enough to congratulate another woman on her successes or to send flowers to her grand opening, but it's not so easy to back your actions with genuine feelings. To truly build a girl gang, we need to build a culture of genuine support between and amongst women. In her 2019 article in *Forbes*, Shelley Zalis insists that "we need to reverse the stereotype that women don't support other women.[5]" Think about it. Betty vs. Veronica. Blair vs. Serena. Katy vs. Taylor. We're confronted daily with fictional and real-life storylines celebrating feuding women and normalizing frenemies. And when we glorify the concept of women vs. women in the media, it's reflected in our real life. It becomes normal to step back into (or continue) our mean girl ways. So let's cheer each other on even when we're not in the same room because women who support other women relentlessly and without boundaries are my kind of women.

---

4   Graham Lauren. (2016). *Talking as Fast as I Can: From Gilmore Girls to GIlmore Girls (and Everything in Between)*. New York, NY: Ballantine Books.
5   Zalis, Shelley. (2019, Mar 6). "Power of the Pack: Women who Support Women are More Successful." *Forbes.com*. Retreivd from: www.forbes.com/sites/shelleyzalis/2019/03/06/power-of-the-pack-women-who-support-women-are-more-successful/#11637f7b1771

2. More Girls in the Gang!

If you own a business, you already know the importance of putting yourself out there, networking, and cultivating meaningful relationships. But you don't need to be an entrepreneur to build relationships—you just need to be committed to trying something new and to reaching outside of your comfort zone and friend group. No one values their close friends more than I do. I know it's important to have that select group of people who get you, support you, laugh and cry with you. But it's also important to have an extended group of friends and peers, and that's where I'm encouraging you to grow. You see, there's a big difference between friends and cliques. Mean girls run cliques. Empowered women build girl gangs! Friend groups only become cliques when it's very obvious that others are not welcome to join.[6] Cliques focus on insider/outsider status and maintaining who is allowed in, in both outward and unspoken ways. A girl gang is not a clique. It's a constantly growing, evolving, and welcoming community for all women. The more welcoming you are, the more people you meet. The more people you meet, the more relationships you build. And the more relationships you build, the bigger your girl gang is!

3. Get Social, Ladies

I'm the first person to #DoItForTheGram. I love Instagram: stories, posts, selfies, shares. It definitely helps that I am also a social media marketer, so I kind of have to love it because it's half of what I do. I know the arguments for why social media is considered a negative: it encourages comparison, we're addicted to scrolling, it can decrease self-confidence. But it's also an incredibly useful tool in building and supporting your girl gang. I've talked a lot about my girl gang being women in business within my local community, but that's only a small piece of the puzzle. The truth is, my girl gang is worldwide. It's my volleyball teammates from college who still cheer

---

6   Gordon, Sherry. (2019, September 30). The Dangers of Cliques for Teens. Retrieved from https://www.verywellfamily.com/dangers-of-cliques-460650.

me on. It's my sister and my cousin whom I still manage to confide in, vent to, and laugh with at least one hundred times per day, despite not living in the same geographic proximity. It's my best friend, whom I physically see maybe twice a year but who has always encouraged my journey. And it's also a number of other women whom I've only met through one social media channel: Instagram.

When I became a new mom, I found it very hard to balance the realities of motherhood and the demands of entrepreneurship. Another woman I follow on Instagram was very public about her struggles in the same area, so I slid into her DMs (p.s. I'm normalizing sliding into DMs as a form of support and community building rather than an oversexualized Urban Dictionary reference. I'm reclaiming DMs. Who's with me?!). So I slid into her DMs and connected with her. Now every so often, we check in with each other, offer support and advice, and know we're not alone in this wild mompreneur journey. She is in my girl gang.

Girl gangs are also built by connecting with women online and then transcending the digital relationship into a real-life one, Look, I fangirl over a lot of accounts. Hello, Jillian Harris, If you're reading this, I am talking to you! But when I think about the genuine connections I've made with other women in business, so many of them started online from a basic interest in their accounts. I've had the privilege to work alongside, create with, and become friends with women whom I once only knew from an Instagram relationship. I recently had the opportunity to participate in a photoshoot (Hello Ottawa's Next Top Model) with an incredible women-led clothing company. The owner of the company, the photographer, and one of the stylists were all from Instagram accounts I had once followed that have transformed into in-person relationships. And, how cool is this, my fellow models were all empowering women from the online sphere with whom I was lucky enough to connect with in person on that lovely day in Ottawa.

On the flip side, I have a close friend who has moved away, and yet she's still one of my fiercest girl gang members. She likes, shares, comments, and cheers on my business from across the country. She asks questions, checks in, and genuinely cares about what's going on in my daily life. So support your girl gang online. Comment on their pics ten times. Tell them they're killing it. Share their work. In the digital sphere, where information can be harmful and negative, do your best to bring sparkle. Be that magic. Build and support your digital girl gang. #GirlGangForLife

4. Building Inclusive Girl Gangs

Here's the thing: we can't actually build a girl gang that supports all women if we're not operating from a space of inclusion. How do we ensure that all women feel included in a girl gang? How do we empower differently situated women in society? As women in positions of privilege and power, we need to do our best to educate ourselves. We have to understand that women of color, LGBTQ women, women who come from poverty are all battling more than just gendered-power relations in our society. I don't want us to revert to a color-blind, 1970s sisterhood in our girl gangs. I want us to be very aware of the real issues that different women face and work hard to celebrate, listen to, and learn about diversity while also promoting inclusion and belonging in our girl gangs. Do you always host your meetings at the same space? Switch it up! Not sure if your language is accessible? Do some research. Looking to build your girl gang? Look outside your immediate circle and comfort zone. There's so much beauty in creating an inclusive girl gang that promotes belonging and more importantly social change. The more inclusive your girl gang, the more rich and powerful it'll be!

5. That Magic of Collaboration

One of the biggest lessons I've learned as a woman in business is that it's okay to ask for help. It's okay to not be the solo star of every project. And it's okay to not want to do it alone. In fact, it's incredible to not only ask for help but to ask other women to join you in your initiatives. It's amazing to be able to work alongside and create with incredibly talented women. And it's a privilege to build and be a part of a girl gang. I believe that when women collaborate and create together, pure magic happens. I'm definitely feeling Candace Okin when she says, "Ladies, it's tough enough out here being Superwoman, and there are certainly enough people who say we can't, WE NEED EACH OTHER!"[7]

* * *

Some of the most incredible experiences I have had as a woman in business have come through collaborations with other women. One experience of community and collaboration that stands out for me was the First Annual MilSpouse Collective Conference.[8] I am a military spouse. Military spouse life is hard. Many spouses, who are predominantly women, face frequent moves, long periods when their partners are gone for deployments or training, and the realities of living in small towns with little to no job opportunities. Couple that with the added obstacles faced by women in business face—yes, milspouse life is hard. My business partner and I started the MilSpouse Collective in hopes of showing other Canadian milspouses the benefits of entrepreneurship and to create a network of support, both professionally and socially. "You're a MilSpouse, That's Pretty Cool" is our slogan. And it is *super* cool. Seventy-five women came together for our first annual conference. Some military spouses shared their experience and expertise by leading workshops, some created on-site experiences for other attendees, and others attended, networked, and built genuine connections. Post-conference we had women build business partnerships, start their own businesses, and strengthen the connections they made that day. We continue to see the beauty of these MilSpouse collaborations every day and for me, it's truly a reason I continue to build spaces that promote community and build girl gangs.

---

7   Okin, Candace. (2018, February 22). Why Women Should Strive to Connect and Collaborate More Often. Retrieved from https://www.livingoverexisting.com/articles/connect-and-collaborate.
8   "The MilSpouse Collective." Retrieved from milspousecollective.ca.

SO LET'S BUILD IT.

Think of all the extraordinary women you know. Think of the women who inspire you. Think of the women you admire. They all have their own girl gang, women cheering them on and supporting them, and they in turn do the same. Shelley Zallis says that "a woman alone has power; collectively we have impact." (Forbes.com)[9]. We need to build and grow girl gangs not only to have an impact on society as a whole but to have a positive impact on each individual member. The Spice Girls were right: girl power is a real thing.

If you asked me what my squad goals are, I'd tell you women who aggressively and relentlessly support each other. Do you remember the scene at the end of *Mean Girls*, when Lindsay Lohan says, "Order in girl world had been restored?"[10] Well, that order is an ending of mean girls and a creation of one large, supportive girl gang. Let's work every day to build our girl gangs, to squash the belief that we need to be in competition with each other to succeed. Let's lead and encourage women to lead by cheering each other on.

I'm building a girl gang—who's in?

---

9   Zalis, Shelley. (2019, Mar 6). "Power of the Pack: Women who Support Women are More Successful." *Forbes.com*. Retreived from: www.forbes.com/sites/shelleyzalis/2019/03/06/power-of-the-pack-women-who-support-women-are-more
10   Messick, Jill (Executive Producer), & Waters, Mark (Director). (2004). *Mean Girls* [Motion Picture]. USA: Paramount Pictures.

CHAPTER 16

LIGHTING THE ROAD TO SELF-LOVE

"To love oneself is to embody the ultimate gift of gratitude for life's unfolding."

JANET MILLER

Janet Miller, divine light activator and conscious grandmother, global energy healer, Reiki master, transformational healer, reconnective healing practitioner, sound healer, and nurse, dedicates herself to raising the vibration of the planet and elevating the consciousness of the people she has the privilege to reach.

Having grown up with addiction, Janet understands how feelings of disempowerment and lack of self-love can impact our lives. She now lives life to the fullest as a champion of fun and games, and she loves to travel and meet new people through her unquenchable thirst for knowledge.

Janet launched her online show, *Own Your Divine Light*, in 2019 and features experts who share wisdom and advice on how to live your genuine life.

Janet finds joy by teaching that self-love is the gateway to our true potential and inner essence. Raising and uniting the planetary consciousness and creating the life and world we have been waiting for is an honor, service, and passion she has embodied.

As a sensitive, empath, truthseeker, and independent spirit, Janet's heartfelt desire is to make a difference and support people in following their dreams and passions.

Janet's most treasured service is being a conscious grandmother to Nathan James, her first grandchild, a young being who has come into a world far more accelerated than the one she grew up in!

https://www.ownyourdivinelight.com
ig: @divinelightactivator | fb: @Janet-Miller-266891874215983

"You find peace not by rearranging the circum-stances of your life, but by realizing who you are at the deepest level." ~Eckhart Tolle

Go in peace! Be at peace! Live in peace!

Quan Yin, the goddess of mercy and compassion, appeared to me in my meditation and said that this is the message I need to give to people: women and men need to make peace between them.

To make peace, we each need to learn to love ourselves again, first through self-love and then through sharing that love with all of humanity. To understand that we are from love is to realize we are all parts of the Creator/Source. Love/Source split us into the male and female expression on this planet in order to experience a physical reality and to know itself in relationship to and with everything around it. What makes us human are our emotions and relationships to everything around us, as well as how we perceive those relationships within us.

The third-dimensional, Piscean Age which valued money, power, and control is over. The polarized beliefs of right and wrong, black and white, strong masculine and weak feminine, which have conditioned our relationship experiences, are being phased out. The Age of Aquarius, the fifth-dimensional age, has arrived, and its values are love, brotherhood, unity, and integrity. This new age of living from the heart is already causing disruptions in how our personal expressions of masculine and feminine natures need to be viewed and respected. This fifth-dimensional age is heralding the peace between us that the Creator/Source desires.

The Age of Aquarius was announced by a 1960s song called "Let the SunShine In" from the musical *Hair*. The song states: "Peace will guide the planets and love will steer the stars. Harmony and understanding, sympathy and trust abound, no more false-hoods or derisions golden living dreams of vision and the mind's true liberation."[1] These words of hope foreshadowed the many changes that are upon us now, bringing to light those characteristics that have stigmatized women, the roles we were expected to perform, and the aggressive ways we have been treated. These issues are being brought to the forefront, promoting the awareness that the Piscean masculine-dominated era is fading away.

To understand the male and female energies within and outside us is a journey, one that deepens our sense of who we are as creator beings and human beings. This knowledge promotes self-love and brings harmony and peace within, which then radiate out to those around us. Self-love is the key and foundation to creating our energetic fields of love. When we love ourselves, we fill our hearts, generating more love for others.

As male and female entities, we have come here to remember who we are: the essence of love. Source energy is love energy. What is our world without love? There is no meaning to life without some form of love!

We now live in a new reality in which we can marry a man/woman, woman/woman, man/man. People are becoming more accepting of the truth that love matters over all else. Source does not judge. Source/God loves the experience of love.

Think of how much love we have in our lives! We love our family, friends, pets, nature, adventure, our community, and our planet! We can also love ourselves, all parts of our light and shadow. Wherever we feel peace and connection, love is there, creating harmony and joy without regard to gender.

Learning to love myself was the foundation to finding inner peace and my true joy in life. But what is self-love? It's the journey inward that opens our heart space. It's time to stop looking out to our physical environment and get intimate with ourselves on this inner journey. Gift yourself moments of stillness to look inward through meditation. The value of meditation is priceless; it

1   Rado, J., Ragne, G., and MacDermot, G.. (1969). Let the sun shine in [Recorded by The 5th Dimension]. On *The Age of Aquarius*. Soul City Records.

provides deep connection and clarity. Meditation opens us to a natural ease and flow to living.

AN INNER JOURNEY EXERCISE

Visualize yourself surrounded in a pyramid of light. It encases you in the light of love. Set an intention to allow only the highest beings or energies of light to be around you. Put your hands on your heart, take a deep breath, and feel this breath enter your body. Feel the flow of breath relaxing your body. Realize your feet on the ground. Imagine the center of the Earth below your feet and feel Mother Earth sending up a golden light through your feet. See that golden light like breath coming through your feet and travelling up through your legs, torso, chest, neck, and up and out through the top of your head. Send that energy, that beam of light, through the roof of your house and out into the sky, and visualize it streaming out into the universe and connecting to the star that is twinkling or calling to you. You are now connected to Earth and to the heavens. Put your hands on your heart, right over left. Imagine the happiest moment you have had in your life. Let that image come up in your mind and then connect it to your heart. What feelings does this moment bring up? Whatever it is—joy or exhilaration—a warmth will permeate through you. Feel it come into your hands. It can be a tingling sensation; if you don't feel it, imagine a warmth or tingling coming into your hands. This is you connecting to your inner essence. Feel the warmth permeate through your body and fill your heart. See it radiating out into a wave of soothing golden light filling your chest, flowing down your legs, into your arms, up your neck, and filling your head and surrounding you in a cocoon of light. This is Source love, loving you! And since we are all aspects of Source being all connected, it is you loving you! Self-love is real!

It doesn't matter whether you meditate for two minutes or sixty. What matters is the concentration of inactivity, giving time to yourself and opening to the serenity of Universal/Source/God energy that richly replenishes us.

* * *

My journey to finding inner peace and self-love meant freeing myself from the constraints of my dysfunctional home at nineteen years old. I had a clear sense of liberating myself. When I left, my world burst open! The freedom and peace of mind I gave myself was priceless. My adventure to regain myself had begun!

Leaving my birth home was the first time I had chosen me, after years of putting everyone else before me. I was ready to discover who Janet was. Our souls create opportunities to find our way back onto our true paths and purpose. This was my chance to find my passion in life, but these occurrences never come in the forms we expect.

Changing our lives starts with recognizing our daily behaviors and becoming aware of their effect on us. These practices have been with us for so long that they are embedded in our unconscious. To undo negative behaviors, we need to bring in fresh ideas and new ways of being.

The new fifth-dimensional frequency exposes our stuck polarity thinking to a new lens.We are poised to envision a new way of thinking and living from the heart. This lens awakens us to the knowledge that we are responsible for our life's journey. If we dig deep to access our wisdom, that effort can reward us with a shift that propels us onto a path of enlightenment. If we have the willingness to be honest and work through the anger and resentments, the blame and shame that keep us stuck, we can release our old beliefs. That's the stepping stone to freedom and self-love.

Once you start this process, the Universe /God/ Source will support you on your journey and the right people will appear to get you through it. As we begin to feel better, we may find that life is taking less effort and bringing more joy.

My own journey has come full circle on this path. I looked at my family dysfunction and realized I was going down the rabbit hole; so I reached out for help. I joined a twelve-step community that became my new family. I regained my self-esteem and found a new passion for life by releasing my shame and blame. My new community opened the doors to a new version of spirituality; I was a nurse when I was introduced to the energy frequencies of Reiki. Reiki filled me with unexpected bliss and joy; my heart opened and I found my truth. I then chose to be an energy conduit and to be of service to humanity in a deep and profoundly new way.

Energy work causes profound shifts in a person's physical, emotional, mental, and spiritual levels. This work helps people release years of pent-up emotions, as I had. It creates deep and lasting changes that radiate out to all those who encounter us. This much-needed clearing promotes feelings of well-being, gratitude, and tranquility: sensibilities that are needed in today's world.

This is the road to peace between the sexes. Our inner peace expands out to all we encounter! Doing the inner work creates a ripple effect. As heart-based, vibrant living becomes our reality, more people awaken to its possibilities and we transform our world. It starts inside and moves outward. By creating this groundwork of self-love, we build strong support for what we choose next in the outer world. The Universe will support us in ways we could never expect, bringing alignment and ease back into our lives. This work engenders feelings of unconditional love between us all and can move us to depths of gratitude never expected.

Women have been the forerunners and have embraced this new consciousness of living from the heart. I've worked with many women ready to shift their lives into more positive thinking and to find their true passions. People who have experienced traumas similar to mine tend to be attracted to this work. A bond of connection and trust is formed, creating a safety net from our shared experiences and opening the door to our healing journey.

Women are seekers, nurturers, and nourishers of life, and they courageously break through barriers. Women have been tasked with hiding their light for centuries, but they are now stepping into the light of healing and loving themselves. Ruth Bader Ginsburg, a U.S. Supreme Court Justice, helped shape the modern era of women's rights. Louise Hay let go of conventional thinking and became dearly beloved by the holistic community. She discerned the connection between disease and our emotional state and how

175

we can change that through daily affirmations. Ellen DeGeneres broke barriers and charted a new path when she came out as gay in 1997 and greatly influenced American attitudes regarding gay rights. Malala Yousafzai, a young Pakistanian woman and advocate for women's education rights, revealed great depths of commitment and courage after almost losing her life when a bomb directed at her went off on her way to school. Pakistan later passed its first Right to Education Bill, making Yousafzai the youngest Nobel Peace Prize winner at age seventeen. Greta Thunberg, who claims autism as her superpower, is fighting for our planet. This sixteen-year-old Swedish Nobel Peace Prize nominee has inspired six million people across a hundred and fifty countries to educate themselves on climate science and to drive their leaders to make immediate changes to our environmental conditions.

These amazing women have shown the world their versatility, courage, dreams, and commitment. Their love of self forms the foundation that carried them through all their trials and with that love as their fuel, they got to expand and thrive. Their lessons and examples show us what it takes to impact change. They showed up, took responsibility, and mastered their experiences, thereby creating peace.

Here's what self-love can do for us:

1. It illuminates the simplicity and lightness that life can embody. As a result, we experience less overthinking and overdramatizing.
2. It helps us gain more inner steadiness and less self-sabotage; our opinions of ourselves go up and we don't crave so much validation and attention from others.
3. It helps us feel more deserving and have more motivation and focus than ever before.
4. We will be happier, and feel lighter. Life becomes more fun when we don't take ourselves so seriously!
5. What has self-love done for me?
6. It helped me release blame and shame when I let go of alcohol and my many self-limiting beliefs.

7. It led me to forgive myself so I could then forgive others.
8. It gave me a new vision of myself and a new mission in life.
9. It opened me up spiritually and led me to become a holistic healing practitioner.
10. It set me on a path I would never have dreamed of through my online show.
11. It created a peace and harmony in my life, as well as a passion and a drive that reignited my joy.
12. It gave me the ability to laugh at myself and know I don't have to be perfect.

These gifts are for everyone! As women, we are being given this chance to reinvent our lives in this new age. We are the way-showers, exhibiting how to balance the inner male and female. Our transparency and willingness to do this inner work is a gift for all.

As all of humanity breaks through the walls of self-limiting beliefs, we open the door to change. Each time we encounter a challenge and push through to the other side, we expand, readying ourselves for the next a-ha moment! We learn a lot from the generosity of those who have struggled and still choose to be of service in the highest degrees of integrity. These masters have gleaned the gold from their life journeys and offer their wisdom and understanding to all who ask. They have become enlightened creators of self-love and mirror it out to the world.

This is our true purpose for being here: to embody love. It begins within us. Loving ourselves will crack our world open in ways we never thought possible.

We are in the Age of Aquarius, when unconditional love, peace, and integrity will become the foundation. Finding peace within ourselves through self-love will help us engender mutual respect between men and women. Our insides will match our outsides, and harmony between the sexes will reign.

Until one can love oneself, how can they truly know love and how to love another? Love is all there is.

I hope Quan Yin approves of this message!

CHAPTER 17

CONNECTION IS THE KEY TO OUR RISING

*"Taking the opportunities to connect
as humans often only requires a
moment and a choice."*

ANNYSE BALKWILL

Annyse is a big believer in the slash life, a concept coined by Brene Brown. As an engineer/mother of two girls/ transformational leadership consultant/yogi/facilitator/business owner/budding author, she practices living a life that challenges her limiting beliefs about who she was, is, and can be. She hopes to live a life that shows her girls how powerful they are and what tremendous choice they have at their fingertips. Annyse's dream for all humans is to know that they are truly powerful, that they matter, and that they have a far greater impact on our world than they could ever possibly imagine. This is her definition of leadership.

The two most important things to Annyse are connection and meaningful conversations.. Connection to self, to one another, and to the collective forms the core of how she shows up to play big in this lifetime. She knows that as more women

connect to themselves, one another, and the greater community, big, beautiful, important

change will happen. She believes it is time for us all to rise. Let's do this, ladies!

www.luminusgroup.ca
ig: @luminus.life | fb:@luminuslife
li:@Annyse Balkwill | t: @luminusgroup

There are almost eight billion of us humans here, cohabitating on Planet Earth. Do you ever wonder why we are here? I think the answer is connection.

When I became a mother to my oldest daughter, Olivia, I brought her home, carried her up our stairs still in her car seat, placed her seat in the middle of our living room floor, and thought to myself, "Who the hell thought this was a good idea? Why am I in these four walls of my house with a brand new human all by myself?" My engineering brain, trained to consider all possible risks when designing water treatment plants, kept wondering who had considered the risk in this. When I brought up my discomfort, though, all I heard in response was, "I did it myself, you will be fine." I can't help but recall the slight bitterness that came with that advice . . .

* * *

I began considering some new questions about community and connection when Olivia was just a wee babe, all while buried in the steep learning curve of becoming a new mother.

What does it mean to be connected?

What does it mean to be disconnected?

Disconnected from what?

The ball really got rolling when I went back to work after a year of maternity leave. After months of waking up early with my daughter around 5:30am, driving forty-five minutes in the dark, dropping her off at an awesome daycare, working for eight or nine hours in the office, picking her up (real close to closing time!), and then a forty-five-minute ride home, followed by dinner, bath, and bed, I began to ask myself, "What am I doing and why am I doing it?"

Important note: I had no shame or guilt about daycare; I was one hundred percent happy to share the parenting load and believe to this day that my children are very fortunate to have many incredible adults in their lives who love them. In fact, this is one of the cornerstones of my belief about connection. Humans need many people in their corner to teach them all the things, and one of the most important things we need to learn is how love can be shown and received in an immeasurable number of ways. I was and am still not equipped to be the sole provider of those experiences for my children, or anyone else for that matter—including myself!

So, back to these questions that really got me going. Why was I working so hard? What was driving me to behave the way I was behaving? I asked why and when I answered, I asked why again and when I answered that, I asked why yet again.

Q: Why am I working the way I work? Why do I respond to my emails so quickly? Why do I say yes to everyone? Why do I work late? Why do I get up early to get to work early?

A: Because I am dedicated to my job. Because I want to do a good job. Because I don't ever want to be the bottleneck. Because I want to help.

Q. Why?

A: Because I want to be reliable. I want to feel valuable.

Q. Why?

A: OMG. Because I want others to validate my worthiness.

This was the truth I had been living. I was looking for approval but it had become buried in my values of being hard-working (which I still think is good when it is clean, meaning no yucky feelings attached to it on any level), dedicated, reliable.

Now I had this ugly monster staring me in the face. This was awareness step one in my mind and led me to my first connection point: I was finally connected to my behavior choices. I was becoming conscious of choices that used to be subconscious in the form of a "should" based on my past experiences. I was beginning to learn a new level of connection with myself. My solution wasn't to quit my job and go find myself. Instead I kept my job and began to get a little more curious about how to connect to myself. I applied curiosity, and when the same old defensive answer came up—"It's just the way I am."—I met that scared part of me with kindness and asked what story I was telling myself. As my journey toward connection continued, it led me to read Brene Brown's *Gifts of Imperfection,* from which I learned to consciously choose to practice working on myself and my thoughts. Each morning I woke up and said, "I am worthy, simply because I am here with open eyes on this day. Everything else is a bonus."

* * *

When I returned to work after having Olivia, I was looking for a better way to connect in many areas of my life, including in meetings at work. My desire for connection at work was mostly a cry for help. The endless meetings I attended and sometimes led had me stating both out loud and in my head, "There has got to be a better way!!" When I shared this thought with my colleagues, I was looking for someone to see me and understand what I was really saying, which was, "Doesn't this mostly feel hollow and like we are going through the motions and not really hearing and seeing one other? And isn't it bothering you the same way it is bothering me?" I never heard the answer I was looking for;instead I was met with people (let's be honest, mostly men) who sometimes literally patted me on the head or shoulder and said, "It's more complicated than that, Annyse." You can imagine my rage followed by disappointment, self-doubt, and hopelessness.

The thing about rising as women is that the opportunity to rise is right here and right now in the place, the job, the life, the family, the marriage, the friendships, the depression, the rut, the mess, the blessings — everything that is part of our lives *right now.* There is no path, no destination, no program, no diet, no mentor, no saving grace coming to whisk you into rising. Don't get me wrong: there are programs, lifestyle choices, and mentors out there that might be for you, but you'll never find *the* mentor, *the* lifestyle, or *the* program. It all starts with a stir, deep inside of us that rises to the surface. The truth we each are seeking is inside ourselves. The desire alone is the way. That first nudge guides us through one tiny baby step at a time.

Leaning into all that I was learning from some powerful authors, the incredible world of the healing arts (I was a brand new baby to this!), and some new concepts about what life might be all about, I began to practice being the person I desperately wanted to find as a "real-life mentor." And it turns out I didn't need someone in my real life as a mentor to get started. I began to apply the small things I was learning to my everyday life, exactly where I was. I would walk into work and declare, "I am grateful for this building, for all the people in it, and I am happy to be here today." I would do this in the front atrium and take in the building's sights and anyone who had been walking by to appreciate it. Of course, I didn't always feel grateful when I arrived at work; there were some rough mornings at daycare drop-off or I would be tired and stressed out about something. But on those mornings, I had to try it anyway, and I did, right from within whatever mental or emotional state I was feeling. I had nothing to lose and from what I was learning, maybe, just maybe, I had something to gain.

I still felt a bit foolish. My engineering/science brain always wants to know the right path prior to embarking on a journey. It also wants to by default know (and by know, I mean judge) that all other routes must be absurd. The haunting voice in my head said, "What if I do this and it fails and I look foolish?"

This fear of looking foolish is closely linked to the seemingly smart label of the skeptic. Our culture feeds us the belief that you must be skeptical, or else you are a fool who deserves all the bad things that happen to you. But to take the next steps I knew I needed to take, I had to do it while feeling all of this yuckiness and fear. I did it quietly on my own at first so I felt safe to be curious, until I began to build my own evidence that my practices were working. This allowed me to release the skeptic over time, at least for this lesson and this moment in time.

Building my own evidence is ultimately what started to connect me to myself again. I began to build trust in myself. I began to be able to do things and share ideas while distancing myself from the impact of what others thought. It was like I could observe their re-actions without taking it personally. The more I understood myself, the more compassion I had for others. The more patience I had for myself, the more I had for others and the more curious I became.

As I followed my curiosity, it led me to the answers about those meetings at work. With the help of an amazing mentor, I was taught how to create an environment in which people can truly connect during meetings of all kinds.

Eventually I couldn't deny the nudges and whispers to bring what I was learning to life, and so I jumped in with both feet and learned how to become the person who can hold space for others to connect during meetings. I began to facilitate meaningful con-versations and quickly realized that we are not so different from one another. The simple fact that we are human is a *huge* base from which we can choose to connect. Taking the opportunities to connect as humans often only requires a moment and a choice. It can be a choice to ask one more question or simply to listen with more empathy and patience.

When we remind ourselves that we have the time we need to be curious when we are prompted by fear—that is the moment and the choice that leads to connection. These moments, these seemingly tiny choices, amplify our lives and the lives of others.

I heard someone once say, "We are only one question away from an interesting story." Each of us has an incredibly inspiring story to share. It could be a big story or a tiny one, a story of tri-umph, sorrow, joy, sadness, anger, lust, courage, or grace. These tiny choices in these tiny moments in time are when we are gifted the opportunity to say to another human with authentic curiosity: "I care about you. I love you. I am here." In asking just one more question, the connection is made. We truly see another human and appreciate their life and their experience. We honor their journey, even for just a moment. From here, the universe responds with a loving, "Hello, my sweet darling, I am so glad you are ready. It is time. Let's get to work and RISE."

So there are nearly eight billion of us on the planet. This means there are billions of people to connect with and unlimited interesting stories to hear. These stories make us all more whole, and we can begin to acknowledge the thread that has us all connected. From there, we can notice the thread that connects us to the Earth, the seasons, the rhythms and timing of the universe, building our faith in ourselves, in one another, and in humanity. When we do this, the rising of us all becomes inevitable.

CHAPTER 18

UNITED WE DANCE, DIVIDED WE CRAWL

"Stars do not condemn other stars for glowing: they just shine."

KRYSTA LEE

Krysta Lee is a singer and songwriter, actor, author, artist, coach, and health and wellness marketing executive who is the proud mama of two beautiful babes (Jaxon and Lillee), and wife to her twin flame, DJ. Her family (and faminals!) live a *modern-day-hippie* lifestyle in Prince Edward County, Ontario, Canada. She's an optimist, a goal-getter, and a big-dreamer who's had a passion for creative writing since her early childhood days.

Living her best life by the motto #SpreadLove, Krysta Lee is all about good vibes and positive energy. She loves her friends, family, fans, and all things animal related. She is a vegan, nature-loving yogi, guided by universal truth which she explores through meditation, channeling, and journaling. She thrives off of being in true states of happiness, health, success, and wealth; and prides herself on working hard (playing harder!), exercising regularly, and expressing gratitude daily.

Krysta is honored to be featured as a contributing author in this book and is exceedingly grateful for the opportunity to be part of such an epic collective and movement alongside such powerhouse women! Empowering female leadership is very important to her because she believes that as women, we have an obligation to make a positive impact on the world. She understands that our future is a direct result of the actions we take today and hopes to inspire as many people as possible with her life's work.

www.KrystaLee.com
ig: @KrystaLee111 | fb: Krysta.Lee.Fanpage | li: @KrystaLee
t: Krysta_Lee | yt: www.YouTube.com/KrystaLee123
IMDB: www.IMDB.me/KrystaLee

There's power in numbers, and we're more effective as a collective. So why do most of us experience so much dividedness throughout our lives, when there could and should be more unity and positive female leadership?

As a woman, have you ever experienced a barrier that makes it difficult for you to connect with some females? Do you ever wonder why it's sometimes challenging to be accepted, respected, or even acknowledged by other women? Have you ever been in the company of females, only to find your genuine efforts fall upon blind eyes, deaf ears, and closed hearts? And as a female, have you ever wondered why it's sometimes easier to get along with guys than with girls?

Yeah, me too. This irks me because I've longed for a deep connection with most everyone I meet, for as far back as my memory goes. Since early childhood, I genuinely wanted to like other people, and have the feeling be mutual in return. My "people pleasing" days began early on, and I'd feel twice as badly whenever said connections were disrupted. This is partially because I'm an empath (I'm sensitive to other people's energy, and often feel what they feel), and I feel better when those around me do, too.

I observed that people are generally happier
when they're getting along in their relations, and
often torn apart and unhappy when they're not.

My first experience with a deep disconnection took place on my father's side of the family, following his death when I was eleven years old. Then came the more common types of divisions with friends and peers throughout my teens and early adulthood, which were inevitable I suppose. In later years, my husband and I had a falling out with some family members from his side shortly after we married. Around the same time, there was another break in my family, this time on my mother's side following the passing of my grandparents. The hardships in my adult life affected me the most, and prompted a big change within.

Life's been tossing curve balls my way since day one, so I've learned to adapt and become whatever I need to be at the time—and this serves me well in connecting with my peers. I've been blessed with many friends from a variety of walks of life. From the "cool kids" to the "underdogs" in school, and the "au-naturel mamas" to the "boss women" in more recent times, I've always felt as though I fit into many tribes. I see little bits of myself in most people I meet, I'm relatable on many levels because of my life's experiences, and I embrace various ways to befriend others.

*If I can help or inspire even just **one** person along their journey, then my mission is a successful one.*

Still, not everyone appreciates that trait of mine . . . and sadly, some even express their disapproval. Since my elementary school days, and continuing all the way until "now-years-old," I've experienced my share of bullying, negative encounters, and grape-vine-gossiping. And time after time, the common denominator within the pattern has been brought on by: *females.*

I lost many friends and family members who silently turned their backs to me after being negatively informed and led by their female counterparts. Most never thought to ask *the other side* of the story—this is how easily people can be influenced. And damn, I admit, I allowed the drama to keep me up at night; in tears, for years. There were times when I thought I wouldn't get up on the right side of the ground, because the consistent confrontations were all-consuming.

"Why was this happening?" I know every one of us is guilty of having a poor attitude now and again; it's human nature, and something we can all work on improving. What I don't get is what's really going on deep down that causes some women to automatically go into defense or offense mode (sometimes without warning or reason), instead of being more transparent, accepting, and non-judgemental in embracing one another.

Is it because women are under a plethora of pressure to look; think; act; and be a certain way, in order to be accepted—so they lash out more easily? Does it have something to do with individual insecurities, through which they see other women as a threat? Are women in some fight-or-flight, self-protection mode based on fear of being judged or cast aside? Why do some women believe when another female gets her shine on, it somehow dulls their glow? Has it been like this since the beginning of time, or is this a new-age pandemic?

I've concluded it's likely a combination of all of the above to a varying degree. And the reason I've experienced this phenomenon again and again is because there's something bigger than myself at work. One of the reasons I'm on this planet is because I'm eager to overcome obstacles, turn wounds into wisdom, and spread love. This is my duty within my destiny, and it's no easy task. Since there's been a devastating amount of disconnect, division, and separation within my circle of female friends and family, I've had many opportunities to learn and grow.

I finally understood a very important life lesson:
Hurt people hurt people.

Read that last bit again. That statement alone changed my perspective of *every applicable person!* No one who's in a good place in their life would ever purposely hurt someone else. People make poor decisions when they're not in their best state of mind, and the choices they make ultimately have no reflection on us. Instead, they highlight that person's own silent screams for help.

These hurting people are the ones who need love most of all. Their negativity stems from a lack of love, a low level of confidence or self-worth, a fear-based mindset, or jealousy and envy. Only unhappy people relish in the hardships of others, and that's not a good way to lead or inspire. Realizing all of this helped me find my way to forgiveness through contemplation and understanding. I've learned to have more compassion, conversations, and eventually celebrations after overcoming it all, too!

This isn't to say that we don't need to establish healthy boundaries with those who hurt us, because we absolutely do. However, I think it's in all of our highest good to try a little more, give a little time to heal, and do everything within our power to work civilly together, unless (and this is a *big* unless!) it's causing a serious disruption to our well-being. Each situation is unique and needs to be addressed accordingly. We *need* to try, yet we *need not* force things.

> ***Big** change had to happen in order to break the cycle of division, and it had to happen **fast.***

These are some practices that worked for me . . .

I slowly proceeded with the rebuilding of several of my broken relationships. I began with imagining myself in the shoes of those who cast stones upon me. I wanted to reconnect with my female tribe whom I loved and adored so much, and I was willing to work to make it happen. I longed to be united once again, and in order to do so, we had to mend the unintentional divide that occurred.

At first I sent love to those I yearned to reconnect with. I wrote letters of clearing and healing, compassion and explanation, gratitude and blessings. Some letters I shared, others I kept for myself; getting it out of my head was helpful. I did my best to communicate as briefly, directly, and gently as possible, and I no longer held on to the words of negativity that came my way. I didn't want the drama to continue any longer, so I adopted the mindset of: if you don't have anything nice to say, just send love.

I made the conscious choice to work on my self-development. I pushed past my comfort zones, pinned my heart back on my sleeve, and took my power back. I relinquished the untruthful rumors, false assumptions, and the negative accusations swirling around me. I reclaimed my inner peace, focused on self-care, and kept myself busy with things that brought joy to my heart and to those closest to me. I did everything in my power to feed "good food" to my soul, and embarked on my own personal growth journey.

I had to get better, to be better. Through trial
and error, I became my own protégé.

I journaled, wrote songs and poetry, and shared inspirational posts on social media that helped me to heal (and to my surprise, innumerable others who were going through similar situations as well!). I painted, meditated, and practiced yoga. I read more self-help books in a handful of years than I'd read in all my previous years combined. I attended workshops, and took courses to further my personal growth. I practiced self-love, and signed myself up to work with several life coaches. I explored and expanded my reality, immersing myself deeply into spirituality. I surrounded myself with only those who accepted me for me, without judgement, which made me feel good inside.

I fully embraced who I was and what I was going through, so I could then thrive and do the same unto others. I worked so hard on becoming a better version of myself that I attracted better versions of other people, too. I filled my cup and was once again able to "poureth over." This is when the magic really took place: in the healing and the coming together afterward. This, my sister, is where we reunited . . . and girl: it felt *SO* good!!

I learned an invaluable life lesson:
Healed people heal people.

As the years passed, one by one we began to have better communications and real breakthroughs. All of us were hurting throughout those times; we all had a desire to be heard, understood, appreciated, and loved. And, we were all very *powerful* women. We began to see past what divided us, and chose to focus on what unites us. It was a slow and sometimes painful process, yet we were able to rekindle our relationships. I'm so proud we stayed the path because I truly believe we are all stronger and better because of it! I can truly thank them for the life lessons they've bestowed upon me, for they helped shape me into the risen woman I am today.

Had none of this happened, I might not have done so much work to heal my past traumas, and perhaps I wouldn't be in this position today: writing a chapter in this book alongside such stellar women. No one needs to go through what we did in order to understand this type of disconnection is not healthy for anyone. No matter what happens between us from here on out, I will always love these women for the lessons of our past, the love and happiness they bring to me today, and whatever gifts they may grace our relations with in the future.

If we all can learn to adopt mutual respect and understanding, regardless of our differences, I truly believe this unspoken disconnect between women would cease to exist!

I believe it is in everyone's best interest to empower, support, and uplift each other. We all come from Divine Source and have contracts to fulfill with "one a-mother." As humans, we have great responsibilities: enforcing a sustainable health plan for our planet, respecting equal rights for all people and living things, recognizing that we are accountable for the future of generations to come, and taking action accordingly.

As women, we have an incomparable gift as the chosen portal between the spiritual realm and this third-dimensional world in which we live. Whether or not we physically bear offspring in this lifetime, I still believe we are here to exemplify this mothering of nature in our own ways. Women contain within them an unparalleled power and ability to literally receive, develop, and deliver new life onto earth, and not a single one of us would be here if a certain "She" did not make it so. Finally, we women who find ourselves in any type of leadership position have a staggering obligation to make a positive dent in this world—and I mean a *big* one!

We must take action with every opportunity we get to make the positive impact that the world desperately needs.

Our personal experiences are our greatest teachers, and as much as this about us as individuals, it's also not. There's a bigger picture happening here. Once we accept that in all areas of life, everything changes, and we can then understand how necessary positive change is for our advancement. My grandfather used to say, "If you're not growing, you're dying!", and this is something everyone could benefit from contemplating.

So let us start with healing, loving, and honoring ourselves. Let us wholeheartedly embrace and empower one another, and set a positive example to inspire change for future females to thrive and do the same. Let us be more like Mother Nature by giving without expectations, and receiving without attachments. Let us live our lives as though someone is always watching us, because (sometimes in mysterious ways), someone always is!

Let us disintegrate our vertical hierarchies and create more horizontal relationships. We rise by using our hands to reach out and lift up our fallen sisters. There are more hands on this planet than there are humans, and we were given two of them for a reason! There will be days when we are the fallen ones, so let's be easy on ourselves and each other. Let us come back stronger, wiser, and better than before.

What else can we do? Serve. Serve yourself, serve others, serve God, serve the Universe. Whatever it is you believe in, just serve. This is how we make a difference, by helping others. This is how we lead, influence, inspire, empower, and thrive. This is how we pave the wave for those to swim the seas, long after our ship has sailed. This is how we ensure that our children, and all future adults in our circles, have a winning chance at a better, more unified and connected life with *all* of their peers. This is how we *live* our legacy now, so we may *leave* a great one when we're gone.

We must be advocates for ourselves, for women,
and for all future females to rise and thrive.

The days of awakening are upon us. We're raising our vibration as a collective of humans, whether we're aware of it or not, so let's make haste and get with the good vibes! Stars do not condemn other stars for glowing: they just shine. Influential female leaders like Mother Teresa don't make history by hating on or dividing from others. They make history because they unite despite their differences, and they exemplify pure and true love for *all* living things. Let's be like the stars, Mother like Teresa, and rock our inner prophet! We all have the ability to practice this divine feminine power.

Women are modern day Goddesses—So let's lead with love, acknowledge our em*power*ment, don our crowns and thrive on our thrones! We can make sweet music as individuals . . . and better still, we can out-play the most intricate orchestra when we come together; each of us contributing our own unique instrument to perform the grandest symphony this world has *ever* heard.

Let's unite and dance, my soul sisters!

May we rise up, put our best boob forward, and
make. Shift. HAPPEN!!

CHAPTER 19

UNAPOLOGETICALLY WOMAN

"Women have traits and characteristics that can be extremely valuable in the corporate context, and we need to learn how to embrace them unapologetically."

LISA J.L. TSAI

Lisa started early in the pursuit of her passion for public service, becoming the youngest political aide to serve in the Taiwan National Security Council. She has held multiple government and private sector roles throughout her professional career, spanning six different countries in Asia Pacific and Europe. Lisa has also advised many Fortune Global 500 companies in her capacity as a corporate financial advisor at HSBC and as a management consultant at McKinsey & Co. She recently left her career at McKinsey to pursue her next goal: helping women achieve financial well-being through her personal and professional experience in finance and management. She currently resides in Sydney, Australia with her partner.

li: @LisaJLTsai

Many women have been inspired by the famous phrase from Facebook Chief Operating Officer Sheryl Sandberg, which encourages women to grab opportunities without hesitation, to press ahead, to project confidence, and to "sit at the table" in order to move up in the business world. But the term "lean In" never really resonated with me. In most corporations even today, senior roles are still held predominantly by men, and in my experience, "finding a seat at the table" often means having to blend in to the big boys' club and show less of our true nature as a woman leader. Personally, I often adapted the way I talked and interacted with my peers as a means to "lean in" to the club—and most of the time, I was remarkably uncomfortable forcing myself to do something outside of my nature.

I started my career in the field of national security. The first official event I attended representing my organization was at an international Air Force defense conference. There were two hundred people, and I could count the number of female attendees with one hand, minus the two fingers wearing jewellery. I was twenty years old, working part-time as the personal interpreter of a retired Air Force General; my job entailed being on stage with him talking about national security policies in front of ex-defense ministers, academics, and politicians from around the world. The weekend before that first conference, I asked my mom to take me to buy the most boring-looking pant suit I have ever seen, learned how to put my hair in a spinster bun, and got a pair of glasses with fake lenses to make myself look ten years older. I had hoped the conference attendees would not notice that I was younger than their daughters, and I had sweaty armpits under a striped blazer that even my grandma would find too dull to wear.

As women, we often try so hard to fit into a world where we think the only pathway to success is the male-dominated circle that does business while sweating together in a sauna or siping $150 glasses of scotch at a cigar bar. We learn how to play golf so we can be closer to the deal circle on the greens; we pretend to give a rat's ass about the difference between a birdie and an eagle, while most of us only care about why Titleist doesn't seem to have the business sense to make cuter clothes for women. However, in my fifteen years in the corporate world, I've slowly come to realize that being a woman doesn't have to be a disadvantage. Many of the characteristics and qualities we exude naturally can become our most valuable assets and our shortcut to becoming a great leader.

UNDERSTAND YOUR VALUE

First, we need to understand who we are and our true value. When I was in my early twenties, I struggled with this. By then I was serving the government, working with the President's National Security Advisor as one of the youngest people to ever work in the Taiwan government as a political appointed aide. There were lots of rumors in the office that I must have had some special relationship with my boss to have gotten the job. Otherwise why in the world would a twenty-two-year-old girl be eligible to be discussing national defense and security cooperation with foreign governments and writing policy papers for the President? It took me nearly a decade to come to peace with the fact that maybe I *was* good enough, that I had the qualifications and skillset to have deserved that job, just like any of my male counterparts. It didn't happen because I flirted with my boss or pulled a Lewinski to secure my position. It happened because I had the language skills required to work with foreign governments and the experience working in a defense and national security think tank—plus I was pretty darn hard-working, with the right attitude that any employer would be lucky to have in their employees!

Whenever you are in doubt about your value, take a step back and look around you. You *are* as good as you think—wait, actually in most cases, we are often *better* than we think. We often hear about how women go to interviews *thinking* they are less qualified than the position requires, whereas men often apply for jobs even if they *are* less qualified than the job requires. We as women need to stop questioning whether we are good enough and instead own the opportunities we have earned for ourselves and feel confident to step up to ones we are qualified to own.

OWN YOUR WOMAN-NESS

Throughout my career, I have often been credited with being a good communicator, very caring, and an empathetic leader: mindful and considerate of other team members. At a risk of generalizing, I think these are traits that many women hold but often are afraid to show too much in the workplace for fear of being labeled as "too soft" or "too emotional." A lot of the time we excel at what we do because of our female qualities, so why do we feel like we need to shy away from being too feminine? When I worked in consulting, every person who joined McKinsey had to take the Myer-Briggs personality test in their first week, and we used the results (our MBTI) religiously throughout our days at the firm as part of our personal identity. Typically, we would be put on a new project every two to three months; in most cases, that meant coming together with a bunch of colleagues we had never met or worked with before. So in order to build an effective working relationship as fast as possible, in the first week of the project we would do a Team Talk in which everyone told one fun fact about themselves and shared their working preferences—and their MBTI. One dimension of the MBTI test measures whether you are a Thinker or a Feeler, and the simplest way to differentiate between the two is whether you make decisions based on logic and facts or on emotions. I was on the far spectrum of being a big "F," and in my first few years at the firm, I often felt this was a liability. I felt I was too considerate of what my clients and colleagues felt, instead of only looking at the facts and numbers and the need to be harsh on my team members when they were underperforming. I told myself that I needed to toughen up.

However, internal McKinsey statistics have shown that while more than half of new members in the firm are measured as being "T," a far higher percentage of consultants who make it all the way to become Partners are in fact "Fs." This shows that either these consultants learn to become more compassionate and perceptive of how others feel in order to become a successful leader or people who are naturally more compassionate and feel for others are more inclined to progress into leadership roles.

Compassion and selflessness are far more important leadership traits than having the most advanced or innovative management skills. In *The Mind of the Leader*[1], authors Carter and Hougaard make a strong case that when we let go of our sense of self-importance, we spend more effort and energy on other people; in this way, you help your people grow and support them in what they need, which in turn lets them spend more of their effort taking care of the customers or doing their job well. Taking care of your employees and being perceptive and supportive of their needs and development allows them to thrive in their space, which is a far more effective management technique than micromanaging their sales plan. However, Carter and Hougard go on to remind us that a leader's selflessness also needs to include confidence. A leader who only tends to the needs of others but does not have confidence in their own direction will run the risk of being a pushover. So feel confident that you can be yourself and embrace your feminine Feeler qualities: selfless and compassionate.

BE YOURSELF AND DON'T APOLOGIZE

Gender is not the corporate world's only diversity issue. Being a five-foot-one Asian female who enjoys having my shellac nails done in different colors and patterns every four weeks, I constantly

1   Carter, J. and Hougaard, R. (2018). The Mind of the Leader: How to Lead Yourself, Your People, and Your Organization for Extraordinary Results. Boston, MA: Harvard Business Review Press.

battle between being true to my identity and trying to make large, tall, white men "take me more seriously." Only recently did I realize that I didn't have to *make* others take me seriously if *I* started taking myself seriously.

For most of my twenties and early thirties, I spent a lot of effort on my appearance; I would never step outside the house without full make-up and hair done. I would even put on some sneaky eyeliner and a dash of blush to go to the gym. I was constantly trying new weight loss methods—oh and trust me, have I ever tried some crazy stuff. If having acupuncture needles inserted all over my belly and thighs while connected to minor doses of electric shockwaves to "kill my fat cells" isn't crazy enough, I'd love to hear what other methods might top it.

I felt better about myself when I had that wing on the tip of my eyeliner or when I was in my five-inch pumps even though it meant my toes constantly felt like they were about to explode. These things made me feel powerful and beautiful, and I assumed they would bring me more advantages in life. As I got older, though, I began to ditch most of that and swung to the other side of the pendulum. I decided that girls who wore make-up to the gym were vain and insecure, and only girls who could face themselves for how they really looked were *real women*, which is what I wanted to be. In reality, I was just tired of always keeping up with my appearance and wanted an excuse I could get myself to buy in to. Being confident and feeling comfortable in your skin is not measured by how much foundation you wear on your face or how much clothing is covering or not covering up your flesh; confidence is a state of mind. It's the mindset of being able to just *be*, feel good about yourself, and be unapologetic about it.

Does this mean I can be obnoxious and self-centred, do whatever I want, and not ever have to apologize about it? I'd say that if those are the values you stand for and the traits that make you feel good about yourself, then sure, go for it—but you will have to bear the consequences of the people and energy that attitude draws you toward. But if being you means being sentimental at work, being caring to your peers even though some will tell you

you're too soft, then *yes*, be yourself and don't apologize. If some days you want to walk around in yoga pants all day and some days you put on fake eyelashes just to go to the supermarket, as long as it makes you feel good, then do it and don't apologize about it. When you are feeling good about yourself, that is when you bring your best to the table. Again, being a selfless leader needs to be combined with confidence—*that's* when you can truly lead with your natural women-ness without fear of being too soft.

* * *

If I had to summarize all of this in one word, it is this: authenticity. Circumstances may require you to adapt to different conditions, but you don't have to change yourself. Women have their own unique strengths and viewpoints that can be incredibly valuable in a corporate context, or in any context for that matter, and leveraging these can enable us to be successful on our own terms. The key is to understand your value, fully embrace your women-ness, and be unapologetically confident in how you use those traits.

I must admit, I'm still figuring it out myself. No one has all the answers to solve the problems in the world that has been dominated and shaped by men for the past six thousand years of human civilization. However, what I do think is important is that we as women all begin to play a part. A part that adequately portrays the other fifty percent of the human population, whether it be in the household, the corporate world, academia, the creative space, or wherever. It doesn't have to be through leaning in and shoving through to the male circles; it can happen simply by being authentic. When we are not afraid of being the women that we are, and leading with those female strengths and characteristics, we can slowly and eventually make women part of the norm.

CHAPTER 20

BORN FOR THE HUSTLE

"Let's lead by rocking our true authentic selves and invite others to do the same."

LOLA T. SMALL

Lola is a global empowerment coach, trainer, and author for girls and women. With over twenty years of combined experience in teacher training, curriculum design, fitness education, athletic event management, and empowerment coaching, Lola is passionate about encouraging girls and women to share their dreams and impact with the world. Certified in life coaching, health & wellness coaching, and personal training, she leads a powerhouse of women in business through FemCity, an international platform dedicated to helping women succeed in business and life.

Through girls and women's empowerment initiatives such as Room to Read, World Pulse, FemCity, and now Let's Woman Up, Lola's work spans from Canada, US, Asia, Africa, and now the Caribbean. As an international best selling author, Lola leads transformative events and retreats around the world, and her ultimate vision is a world filled with girls and women who are strong, confident, and making a difference.

Her next book, Dear Money, I Love You, is set to publish Spring 2021.

She currently lives in Ontario, Canada with her family.

www.lolasmall.com

ig: @lola.lets.woman.up | fb: @lolatsmall | li: @lolatsai

Drive. Ambition. Motivation. Whatever you want to call it, I have grown up with it: it's a part of me.

I grew up as a girl in Asia, a place where boys are historically favored as the torchbearers of the family name. Our family was an extraordinary one, as my two sisters and I were lucky enough to have had a different destiny than the girls around us.

My family and I are from a tiny town in southern Taiwan, a small but mighty island south of Japan, so it was a huge deal when we moved to the U.S. when I was eleven. My dad's biological family had ten kids and he was the youngest. Even though the family was fairly well off, by the time they had him, they were struggling financially. His parents decided to give him up for adoption to a couple from the same town, and he grew up alongside his biological siblings but with much less privilege and opportunities. His entire life, he had to create his own path and prove to himself and the world that he was worthy. Wanting better education and a different future for me and my sisters, even when others scoffed at how much he was investing in us *girls*, he made it happen and moved our family to the U.S when he was thirty-six, changing the trajectory of our lives. My dad didn't believe in us settling early for a life of marriage and babies simply because we were born female; instead, he chose to create a new path for us to discover our own destinies and fulfill our potential.

Fresh off the boat in Oregon at age eleven, I had to learn my ABCs fast so I could become the spokesperson for my family. When things didn't work out in the U.S. as my Dad had hoped, my family returned to Taiwan when I was fifteen, but we decided that I would stay in the U.S. to finish high school. I had to figure out very quickly how to lead myself. All I remember from that last day of saying goodbye to my family was the quiet and awkward mumblings of a "bye" and "take care of yourself,"—it was not the norm for Asian families to show much emotional affection through hugs and "I love you's."

I eventually went to Canada for university, returned to Asia, and then immigrated back again to pursue my passion for personal growth and empowerment work. I have found myself over and over again in life stages that require me to step up and create my own path, and it has become clear to me that I have been given this life to carve out my own unique journey with what I have been given. No one holds the reins of my life but me. My desire to give back to my family for having sacrificed a tremendous amount of emotional strain and financial support to see me succeed has made me hustle.

Today I am motivated, driven, and ambitious, because that's how my life has shaped me. Through all the stages of my need to find myself so I could survive on my own and carve out my own path, I have grown to love who I am. It has since become a passion of mine to encourage other women to find the same fire within themselves: to shine, to feel the power of their potential, and to fully love who they are. This is my purpose in this lifetime.

IT ALL BEGINS WITH THE SELF: SELF LEADERSHIP

The very first self-help book I ever read was *The 7 Habits of Highly Effective People* by Stephen Covey, which inspired a deep journey of introspection and pursuit of self-understanding in my early twenties. One concept that really struck a chord with me was that of conscious personal choice, which has become a guidepost in how I choose to lead myself:

> Look at the word responsibility—"response-ability"—the ability to choose your response. Highly proactive people recognize that responsibility.

> They do not blame circumstances, conditions, or
> conditioning for their behavior. Their behavior is a
> product of their own conscious choice, based on
> values, rather than a product of their conditions,
> based on feeling.[1]

This principle made me see that regardless of who we are and what we are up against, we can always choose how we act and react. This intrinsic control and power means that no one is in the driver's seat but us. What an eye-opening truth with which to see and approach life!

My father could have held a grudge about his childhood, but instead he chose to better ours. I could have let myself wallow in sadness or insecurity when left on my own at fifteen, but I used it to my advantage to have a wonderful time in high school and to strengthen my sense of self. I felt strong and powerful because I could shape myself however I wanted, with no one telling me what to do or how to be. I tackled my personal growth like a nerd on a special school project and read ferociously all the self-enrichment books I could get my hands on. I analyzed myself, asked deep questions, took inventory of personality traits and personal values. And most important of all, I got clear on what it is that I wanted to dedicate my life to and how I wanted to make a difference in this lifetime.

In the summer of 2007, while I was living in Taiwan, a friend from Canada invited me to join her in the Philippines for a vacation, an experience that would deeply impact my life. I had suggested that we do something meaningful with our time there, and we decided on and coordinated a body-mind-life empowerment workshop for fifty-two girls at a boarding school that took in underprivileged kids and orphans in Manila. The small, bare classroom was packed with girls ages nine to seventeen; many were eager and excited for us being there, while others were hesitant and skeptical of what the two of us were up to. The day was filled with personal discovery games and activities, with sporadic emotional moments in which

---

1   Covey, S. (1989). The 7 Habits of Highly Effective People. New York, NY: Free Press.

we learned about the girls' lives, and a brief tour of the long hall filled with single beds and tiny shelves that the girls called home. To add to the overwhelming feelings we had already experienced throughout the day, the girls gifted us their thank-you by singing Josh Groban's song "You Raise Me Up." Thinking of the ugly cry we cried that day makes me teary all over again!

This almost-out-of-body experience became a pivotal moment for me: my entire Being knew and felt that *this* was what I was put on this Earth to do. To connect with girls and women, to be a reflection for them to be seen, to remind them of their value and worth, and to inspire them to share their greatness with the world. I had seen and felt my spark in igniting someone else's, and I was hooked.

Each of us has this ability to search within ourselves, see how we want to show up for the world, and in the process of sharing, impact someone else. Our self-leadership then becomes a gift to the world.

SHARE YOUR PASSION LIKE WILDFIRE: WE CAN INSPIRE OTHERS

It is so extremely special to have been born a human being, especially a woman, in this particular time in history when humanity is in much turmoil. We could've been born a little bug, or a tree, or anything else that takes up space in this vast Universe. But the fact that we were born a sentient being, with a powerful mind that can make decisions and a palpable heart with emotions as moving as ocean waves means that we have tremendous power within us to create massive change. We have complete free will to design our own reality, shaping everything that is within our reach and affecting other humans around us through our thoughts and feelings.

As women, our natural inclination is to share, connect, bond, and collaborate . . . qualities that build vast webs and create contagious energy, which gives us a powerful advantage as leaders in all corners of our world. Whether you are in charge of your little home, the big corner office, your classroom of rowdy teenagers, or a community of change-makers, your ability to see the connection between another person and yourself is your greatest asset in being able to relate, influence, and inspire. And when we add what we love to the mix, this combination of connection and passion truly makes our world go around.

I didn't become a leader intentionally; I stepped into the role when I sought out support and community for myself when I was ready to return to the entrepreneurial world after the birth of our son. My husband and I had moved across the country for his new job, and my lack of a network didn't affect me too much until our son turned two and I was ready to re-launch my coaching business. I panicked at the fact that I didn't know a single soul in the local business community, and definitely no one knew of me, so instinctively, I knew I had to look for two things: like-minded women and a way to be in the community. Soon enough, I was leading a collective of twenty-five like-minded women in business as a mastermind through a global women's organization called FemCity, and my personal success, as well as the success of the women in the group, skyrocketed. We have built beautiful relationships, supported each other in our personal and business lives, and created a strong presence in our city as a source of support and empowerment for other entrepreneurial women. What a transformative experience and journey it has been!

Leadership comes from our deep knowing that all of us are one and the same and that by connecting our strengths, talents, and visions together, we can inspire and uplift each other to do phenomenal things. My biggest love and passion is to empower women to see their highest potential and to encourage them to express and use it for the betterment of our world. Taking that passion and promoting it like wildfire is my form of leadership. There's no hierarchy of me being better than you and telling you what to do. It's just me sharing my heart and vision with yours so that we can join forces and do it together. The synergy that women can share and build with others is a loving, nourishing, and productive energy that gets shit done. We don't need official titles or fancy projects to put ourselves in leadership roles; we need women who use their own fire within to spread their passion to others and ignite more fires for positive social change.

At this crucial point in time, the world needs us to amplify this type of leadership to reach a critical mass for more love and unity on our planet. As long as you are a human being, male or female, you have a mind and a heart that is available for establishing understanding, connection, encouragement, and collaboration. You are a leader and you can change the world. Let's use our gift of sharing passion with each other to amplify our leadership!

REFUELING THE ENERGY: LET'S KEEP BUILDING MOMENTUM

As I type these words, my body is tired and I am fighting a head cold. I am a busy mama with an active toddler, wrapping up a part-time job while running a business, cranking out a few books, leading a community of women, and let's not even talk about keeping up with social media, folding the laundry, and having a decent relationship with my husband. Fueling our passions and our visions and inspiring others to do the same demands an overwhelming amount of energy, in addition to keeping up with the day-to-day. Women are known to juggle multiple balls in multiple courts, so we must have strategies and systems in place to make sure we take care of our own wellness and are fueled and recharged to keep the drive going. Choosing to consciously share our passion and ambition with the world requires us to pay attention to our energy and nurture it well so that it can serve us and others for the long run.

By immersing myself in positive and uplifting circles of women through my FemCity community and fellow authors from collaborative book projects, I am refueled and supported by like-minded women who remind me of my power. Having fun ladies' nights to laugh, eat, and drink, as well as discuss goals, dreams, and struggles, helps me to stoke the fire within to get up the next day and move forward. Find your communities of people who give you strength and help you recharge.

I also remind myself of the legacy I want to leave through the words in the books I write and the philanthropic efforts I hope will help to love the world. Thinking of ways I can contribute to positive social change rekindles my motivation and keeps my momentum going. As long as I am breathing, I want to be of use to humanity and fulfill the purpose I was given by being here as a sentient being. Keep your legacy goals front and center as a reminder for yourself that your actions have a bigger purpose than yourself.

Coming back to the center of myself, I make sure I implement non-negotiables to maintain and maximize my personal energy. I center myself by writing in my journal, I tap into my creative flow by taking walks and going for runs, and I power up my momentum with strength training sessions, even if only for fifteen minutes after everyone has gone to sleep. Create non-negotiables in your daily routine that help you stay focused, on track, and revved up!

My life trajectory has taken me on a journey that I couldn't have ever anticipated. From living in a tiny little island town to reaching the world through my written words, my search for my self and for the light in another person's eyes has fanned my fire for what I know is possible for all of us women. Through our hearts and muscles, we are here to light the way for the world by sharing our passionate and powerful selves.

My heart and muscle is how I hustle. This is what I was born for. This is what you were born for.

Let's get in on this hustle, together, and change the world.

ACKNOWLEDGMENTS

"To my amazing parents, broski, family, my soul sisters and brothers, those who have lifted me up, trusted me, cheered me on, the vision-casters, and to my world: Jon and Cole."

~Natalie Zombeck

"To my friends and family for tolerating my growing pains, my mentors for your patience, my other half for being my rock and partner in crime, and to all the women that keep me inspired."

~Sarah Yeung

"To my husband, Spencer. I couldn't have picked a better partner. To my 3 beautiful children, Lily, Adrian and Zoey, you are what inspire me to be the best version of myself. I love you all beaucoup."

~Pamela D'Ippolito

"Thank you to my husband, Ryan, for always believing in me, for holding our vision together close to his heart, and for truly being a partner. I'm forever grateful for you."

~Christina Whiteley

"For every girl who dreamed of greener grass, and to everyone who helped me realize that the grass is greener where I chose to water it."

~Annie Ngu

"I am forever grateful to the people in my life who believe in me and inspire me to dream bigger every day! Thank you! "

~Theresa Toscano

"To my parents, Donna and Ross, for raising me the way you did. My brother, Todd, for being my forever constant. To Andy Vince for believing in me. To my husband, Dan, you are my everything."

~Lori Hicks-Armitage

"Thank you to my parents, siblings, my love, Jay, and my greatest masterpieces; Aaliyah and Roland. To my besties; Krysta, Val, Adele, Dianne, Ness, and Cal. To Lola, our fearless leader, and GBR for bringing this book to life. This is dedicated to my Dad, Castro Kelly."

~Steph Clark

"To my amazing family and friends who encouraged me through the years. Much love to my parents and two children, Chantelle and Mark. Kudos to Lola, Ky-Lee, and the GBR team, where authentic stories are shared by women for the benefit of all."

~Lisa Pinnock

"To my husband, Johnnie, my parents, Alvin and Ara Bell, and my Goodwill family, Chris, LaRita, and the board members and staff. You are my 'hub of possibility'. To my Fem sisters, Lola and Natalie. To Jean Veatch who insisted I take this step."

~Shell Richardson

"Women leaders that inspire my passion, Maria Montessori, Princess Dianna, and Grace Vickerman. My family, Leo and Darcy, and my friends, and my staff for letting me be who I am and helping me shine."

~Sally Lovelock

"To my parents, my brother, my husband, and friends for supporting my dreams. To my team in my career. To my family pets, you have taught me what it truly means to make it about others before myself."

~Michaella Putman

"Thank you to Lola for your vision, and GBR for bringing this book to light. Thank you to my life partner, Steve, and mostly to my babies, Rowan and Arion for opening me to grow into the woman writing these words."

~Elizabeth Meekes

"To my mom and aunt Tina, my husband, Jeremy, to Emily, and my three kids, Ryder, Payton, and Nash. You all inspire and support my crazy ideas and dreams."

~Julia Lefaivre

"To my own girl gang for supporting me and showing me community; Christina, Renee, Dana, Chrissy, Pam, Katie T. and Katie B. To my partner, Dan, and my son, Hnerik, for showing me how to live. In loving memory of Baba."

~Jessica Khouri

"Thank you to my grandmother, Magdalena Kozlowski; at nineteen, she had the courage to cross the ocean alone to freedom. Her courage showed me that the journey to freedom is through self-love."

~Janet Miller

"I wouldn't be on this journey without the support of my brilliant best friend and business partner, Kathy B. Thank you to Natalie Z. for introducing me to Lola! And to Kelly G. and Kate Q. for being the first to read my chapter and offering support."

~Annyse Balkwill

"To my dear friends and family who support and encourage me every day: thank you. Thanks to my fierce female tribe: Steph, Lola, Ky-Lee, and the GBR team. Infinite love and gratitude for my babes Jax and Lil, and my hubby DJ. I'm better than who I was before you came along, because you came along."

~Krysta Lee

"I want to thank my parents and sisters who have always supported me in all of the choices I've made in life, even when they didn't always make sense. They trusted me to be the best of who I am. I also want to thank my partner, Jens, who accepts and loves me for exactly the way I am."

~Lisa J.L. Tsai

"Thank you to all the strong women in my life who have shown me that being true to our authentic selves is the way to lead the world. Special gratitude to FemCity Founder, Violette de Ayala, and GBR Founder, Ky-Lee Hanson, for creating space for women to shine. To my sisters, Lena and Lisa, and all my girlfriends around the world for being a part of me."

~Lola T. Small

Check out some of our other titles

www.goldenbrickroad.pub

Shop at 20% off with promo code GOLD20

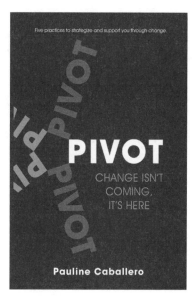

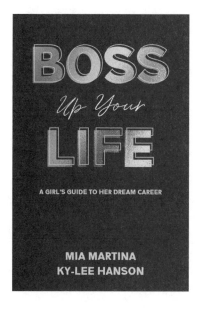

Check out some of our other titles

GOLDEN BRICK ROAD
PUBLISHING HOUSE

Link arms with us as we pave new paths to a better and more expansive world.

Golden Brick Road Publishing House (GBRPH) is a small, independently initiated boutique press created to provide social-innovation entrepreneurs, experts, and leaders a space in which they can develop their writing skills and content to reach existing audiences as well as new readers.

Serving an ambitious catalogue of books by individual authors, GBRPH also boasts a unique co-author program that capitalizes on the concept of "many hands make light work." GBRPH works with our authors as partners. Thanks to the value, originality, and fresh ideas we provide our readers, GBRPH books are now available in bookstores across North America.

We aim to develop content that effects positive social change while empowering and educating our members to help them strengthen themselves and the services they provide to their clients.

Iconoclastic, ambitious, and set to enable social innovation, GBRPH is helping our writers/partners make cultural change one book at a time.

Inquire today at www.goldenbrickroad.pub